I have known Patricia King for many years. I have learned from her the importance of decreeing, not just praying. Decreeing the Word of God in faith over yourself, your family, and your business is an important activity for every Christian. By continuing this discipline along with fervent prayer, you build up your own spirit and provide a doorway for the Holy Spirit to move in your life. Decreeing God's Word over your life regularly empowers you to face difficult situations with His wisdom and love on a daily basis. I recommend that you read Patricia King's book *31 Decrees of Blessing for Your Life* and discover a new realm of spiritual life and power.

JOAN HUNTER
Author, evangelist
Founder and president, Joan Hunter Ministries

What an amazing book! *31 Decrees of Blessing for Your Life* will not only transform your thinking, it will release God's blessing and goodness into every area of your life! There's nothing more powerful than speaking and declaring what God says about you. Patricia King's decrees, based on God's Word, will release faith, hope, and love into every situation you face and will cause you to experience the blessed life God created you to have. This is a book you will read over and over again.

MATT SORGER
Author of *Power for Life*, TV host, prophetic healing revivalist
mattsorger.com

When you bought this book, it likely was because you, like me, have learned to trust the author. You expected a good daily reading for inspiration. What a surprise to open the cover and discover you were looking into God's toolbox for building a successful life. No tool missing and explicit directions for completion make this little book become a large bargain.

DR. IVERNA M. TOMPKINS
Author and Pastor Emeritus at Church for the Nation
Phoenix, Arizona
Iverna Tompkins Ministries

My dear friend Patricia King has so powerfully grasped the invitation the Lord has given each of us to decree a thing so that it would be established. God truly wants to bless us, and *31 Decrees of Blessing for Your Life* uplifts as it encourages us to meditate on, proclaim, and activate the Word of God—daily—in our life and in the lives of those around us.

DR. CHÉ AHN
Apostle, Harvest Apostolic Center, Pasadena, California
Apostolic leader, HRock Church
President, Harvest International Ministry
International chancellor, Wagner Leadership Institute

Patricia has found an amazing truth that will empower all those who will make it their own. When the redeemed choose to agree and decree God's Word, they can activate the will of God with the fruit of their lips. The kingdom of God is activated.

Choose your words wisely and release the established will of God over your life with the declarations in this book. Never has it been so easy to position yourself for greatness!

DR. CLARICE FLUITT
Author, prophetess, motivational speaker

Scripture proves the extraordinary power and effectiveness of making decrees. I absolutely love this book because Patricia has done the hard work for us by formulating solid biblical prayers that will produce a manifestation of everything from favor to health and healing. Within this cover are 31 days of powerhouse decrees that will bring YEARS worth of divine promises into your life! When I began to decree one chapter every day over my own household, I saw fruit immediately! You must get this book.

KATIE SOUZA
Founder of Katie Souza Ministries

If you want to see the blessings of God unlocked in your life, Patricia King's new book *31 Decrees of Blessing for Your Life* is a must for you to read. We have seen nations impacted, laws changed, financial breakthrough, debts canceled, families come into revival and blessing, and so much more as we made decrees. In this book you will truly learn how to call forth "that which is not" into your daily life and see the blessings of God explode in your walk with God! We highly recommend Patricia King's book for you and all your loved ones.

JERAME AND MIRANDA NELSON
Living at His Feet Ministries
livingathisfeet.org

31 DECREES OF BLESSING

FOR YOUR LIFE

PATRICIA KING

BroadStreet
PUBLISHING

BroadStreet Publishing® Group, LLC
Savage, Minnesota, USA
BroadStreetPublishing.com

31 Decrees of Blessing for Your Life

Stock or custom editions of BroadStreet Publishing titles may be purchased in bulk for educational, business, ministry, fundraising, or sales promotional use. For information, please e-mail info@ broadstreetpublishing.com.

Cover design by Chris Garborg at GarborgDesign.com
Typesetting by Kjell Garborg at GarborgDesign.com

Printed in China
18 19 20 21 5 4 3 2

Contents

INTRODUCTION

The proclamation of decrees based on Scripture has revolutionized my life and ministry. I have experienced increase and multiplication of blessing in every area of my life since regularly decreeing positive faith-filled words of truth. As I have shared with others this treasured tool for success, the effect and influence of God's goodness on their lives have been remarkable.

The word *decree* is a legal term that can mean

- an authoritative instruction provided by someone who has authority or by a government.

- a judgment decided by a court of law.

The words we speak have power and can potentially create life or death (James 3:5–10). But when we make a legal proclamation that comes from God Himself, we are then operating in a power that trumps all other power.

Jesus said, "The words that I speak unto you, they are spirit, and they are life" (John 6:63 KJV). His words are filled with power and have the ability to create His kingdom's glory in the earth. When you proclaim God's Word in faith, it is activated to bring about His will and purpose for your life.

Examine the following encouraging Scripture to see how powerful His Word is: "For the word of God is living and active and full of power [making it operative, energizing, and effective]" (Hebrews 4:12 AMP).

When you decree God's Word, it is alive and full of power and brings itself to pass. According to Isaiah 55:11, it does not return empty but accomplishes everything it is sent to do. God's Word is the final authority. If He said it, He will make it good!

In the book of Job we find this profound and powerful statement: "Decree a thing, and it will be established" (Job 22:28). In Esther 8:8 we read, "A decree which is written in the name of the king and sealed with the king's signet ring may not be revoked." Jesus, our eternal King, has given us all the glorious promises in the Word. They are for every child of God to enjoy.

When you decree these blessings in faith, it is like building a framework in the spirit realm that the power of God then fills with a manifestation of the promise. The Word you decree attracts the manifestation of what has been proclaimed. Every word you decree has power.

This book is designed to inspire you with a daily devotion for every day of the month, which will turn your attention to the heart of God and His wonderful intentions for your life. Each devotion is followed by ten powerful decrees that are based on the Word of God. The Scripture references are also available for you after the decrees to read individually if you desire. This will help you receive full impact from them as you meditate on the truth they contain, allowing them to renew your mind. Finally, there is a daily activation for you in response to each devotion and decree. Acting on the Word of God helps seals it in your heart and life.

Watch transformation take place as you daily give Him your focus. Use this book to bless every aspect of your life.

Here are some benefits that await you as you give God's Word your focus:

- The Word you meditate on and decree will not return void but will accomplish everything it is sent to do (Isaiah 55:11).
- Your decrees of the Word will frame the will of God over your life, allowing the Spirit to fill the framework and manifest results (Hebrews 11:3).
- The word you proclaim will dispatch angels to labor on your behalf as you become God's voice for His Word to be released in the earth (Psalm 103:20).

- Your decrees of the Word will send forth light that will penetrate darkness (Psalm 119:130).
- Blessings will be attracted to you as you proclaim in faith the promises He has given you as a believer.
- You will create in your life and in the earth what was not present previously through faith-filled decrees (Romans 4:17).
- The Word proclaimed functions as a weapon of spiritual warfare and secures victory for your life (Ephesians 6:10–20; 2 Corinthians 10:3–5).
- Your decrees of God's Word will empower and strengthen you (Ephesians 3:16).
- The Word decreed is like seed that goes forth and brings a harvest for you according to the nature of the seed (Mark 4).
- Sanctification (setting you apart for God and His purposes) is activated through the proclamation of God's truth declared over your life (John 17:17).

My prayer for you as you walk through this 31-day devotional of decrees is for your life to be enriched with the full manifestation of every decree. You are deeply loved with God's extravagant affection, and God has purposed for you to be blessed beyond measure. May His blessings truly come upon you and overtake you (Deuteronomy 28:2). Enjoy your glorious journey of transformation as you experience His blessings upon blessings.

PATRICIA KING
Author, motivational speaker
PatriciaKing.com

DAY ONE

BLESSED WITH LOVE

"I have loved you with an everlasting love;
Therefore I have drawn you with lovingkindness."

JEREMIAH 31:3

God truly loves you with an everlasting and unconditional love—He really does! First John 4:8 teaches that God *is* Love! Love is a Person and He created you in His image and likeness, filled with love. Everyone needs love because we were created for love and by Love.

When mankind fell into sin, we became separated from God—separated from perfect Love. As a result, we experienced guilt, shame, fear, and condemnation, but this was never God's intention or desire for us. We walked away from perfect Love.

Through Christ we have been restored to God. "For God so loved the world, that He gave His only begotten Son, that whoever believes in Him shall not perish but have everlasting life" (John 3:16). Even though we turned our hearts against Him, He never abandoned us. He never stopped loving us. Instead, He put a plan into place that would restore us to back to Him—to Love.

God's plan was brilliant. He knew that we did not have the ability to make our wrongs right. We owed such an enormous debt because of our sins that it was impossible for us to pay it back. As a result, He decided to pay the debt for us.

God decided to become man and pay the debt in full. Jesus Christ came as a man and obeyed and fulfilled all the law and commandments on our behalf. He never sinned. He was perfect. He then chose to absorb all of mankind's sins as He hung on the cross. He died and paid the penalty for all of our sins and transgressions. He actually became sin, and in exchange He gave us His righteousness.

What an extravagant gift. In order to receive this love that will never weaken, fade, or diminish, we simply receive Him into our life as our Savior and Lord by faith. He did all the work to restore us to God—to restore us to Love. All we have to do is believe.

This love is not based on your ability to obey His commandments, your behavior, or your performance. It is based on His unconditional love for you—for us. He will *always* love you! You are His dear child. You are His beloved. You are His precious one and always will be. When you receive and understand this great and glorious love, then it is easy to love Him in return with all your heart, mind, and strength.

"See how great a love the Father has bestowed on us, that we would be called children of God; and such we are" (1 John 3:1).

DECREES

I DECREE THAT:

1. I am loved with an everlasting love, and with lovingkindness God has drawn me to Himself.
2. I bask in this love and nothing whatsoever will ever separate me from this love God has poured upon me.
3. God's love for me never fails; it is rich and forgiving, so gentle and kind.
4. God's love is over me as a banner that gives me covering and victory, leading me in the way I should go.
5. I follow after Him because He draws me with His intimate love.
6. I have been called to know this rich love that surpasses knowledge so that I am filled with His fullness.
7. I truly am the object of His deepest love and affection!
8. Because of His love for me, I will never perish but will have everlasting life with Him.
9. The love of God wells up within me like fresh rain from above and overflows me with perfect peace.
10. The Lord pours His unfailing love upon me daily, and as a result I am able to love others freely.

Decrees based on the following Scriptures: Jeremiah 31:3; 1 John 3:1; Romans 8:38–39; 1 Corinthians 13:4, 7–8; Song of Solomon 1:2, 4; 2:4; Ephesians 3:18–20; John 3:16; Psalm 42:8; Luke 6:35

ACTIVATION

Be still for a few moments and savor the love that God has for you. Meditate on His kindness and tender mercies that He constantly blesses you with. Listen for Him to speak to your heart as He speaks, into your thoughts, how much He loves you. Journal your thoughts—and journal *His* thoughts.

_____

_____

_____

_____

_____

_____

_____

_____

_____

_____

_____

_____

_____

BLESSED WITH FRUITFULNESS

God blessed them; and God said to them, "Be fruitful ..."
GENESIS 1:28A

God loves you and desires you to be blessed with fruitfulness in every area of your life. Right in the very beginning of the Bible we see His heart for mankind: "and God said to them, 'Be fruitful.'" He wants you to enjoy fruitfulness. He created you for this very purpose.

Take a moment and imagine yourself overflowing with fruitfulness in everything you put your hands to. Yes, everything you touch is blessed! Your family life bears fruit, and your provision bears fruit and increases; you are fruitful in your workplace and in all your relationships. This is truly God's will for you!

In John 15:5, Jesus taught His disciples a secret from the Father concerning fruitfulness. He said, "I am the vine, you are the branches; he who abides in Me and I am in him, he bears much fruit, for apart from Me you can do nothing."

I once had a lemon tree in my yard that produced lemons that were enormous and plenteous. There were so many lemons on the tree that the branches would sometimes break due to the weight. They were loaded with fruit! The branches in and of themselves had no ability to produce those glorious lemons. They simply hosted the fruit. If I cut off a branch and put it on my table and commanded with all my might, "Produce lemons," it would not produce even one lemon—no matter how hard the branch might attempt to comply. Why? Because it was not attached to the tree. On its own it can produce nothing. It must abide in the lemon tree to produce fruit.

This is a picture of you and me when we are in Christ. Jesus Christ is the life-giving tree. You become a branch in this glorious tree when you invite Him into your heart to be your Savior and Lord. He comes by His Spirit and lives in you when you ask Him with sincere faith, and your life is then in Him. His life-giving Spirit living in you produces fruit. You don't need to strive or worry. You simply need to believe with joyful expectation that what God promised you, He will fulfill. You are destined in Him to bear fruit—much fruit!

DECREES

I DECREE THAT:

1. I am truly blessed with a fruitful life.
2. I am like a tree that's firmly planted by streams of living water with green, healthy leaves producing fruit in due season.
3. I am not anxious when there is lack all around me and when times seem difficult, because I am a fruitful vine, always producing and bearing good fruit.
4. I flourish like the palm tree.
5. I continue to grow strong and upright in my life and faith.
6. I will still yield fruit in old age, and I will be full of abundance, energy, and vitality because the fruit of righteous is a tree of life.
7. I abide in Christ, and therefore I manifest the fruit of the Spirit: love, joy, peace, patience, kindness, goodness, faithfulness, gentleness, and self-control.
8. The fruit I bear in my life is better than gold and the choicest silver.
9. The fruit of Christ's light in me consists of goodness, righteousness, and truth. I am fully satisfied with good by the fruit of my words, and the deeds of my hands return to me.
10. I am destined to bear good fruit because of God's faithful love for me.

Decrees based on the following Scriptures: Genesis 1:28; John 15:5; Psalm 1:3; Jeremiah 17:8; Psalm 92:12, 14; Proverbs 11:30; Psalm 23; Proverbs 8:19; John 15:16; Colossians 1:10; Galatians 5:22–23; Ephesians 5:9; Proverbs 12:14; 13:2; 18:20–21

ACTIVATION

Take some time to be aware of areas of fruitfulness you already see in your life and thank the Lord for these wonderful things. Then ponder areas of your life that lack fruit, and journal prayers to God regarding where you would like to see increased fruitfulness.

DAY THREE

BLESSED WITH A BLESSED LIFE

"All these blessings will come upon you and overtake you."
DEUTERONOMY 28:2A

Close your eyes for a moment and imagine yourself literally being overtaken by blessings. A great example of this picture is that of a football player being aggressively tackled to the ground from behind. In this same way, God wants you to be overtaken by blessings. God is a blessing God, and He wants you blessed beyond measure! You were created to live an extremely blessed life!

The word "blessing" has several meanings, including an authorization that assists or permits you to do something, authorization and assistance from God, a gift, good fortune, or something that is beneficial or contributes to happiness.

When Jesus came to the earth, He began His ministry by preaching, "Repent, for the kingdom of heaven is at hand" (Matthew 3:2). The kingdom of heaven is a realm and dimension of blessing, and its atmosphere is love. The Bible teaches much about heaven. It is beautiful and glorious; full of God's presence, angelic activity, and joy; and absent of pain, sorrow, lack, sickness, and death.

It is God's desire that in and through Christ we live in this dimension of blessing while on the earth. Jesus taught us to pray in this way: "Your kingdom come. Your will be done, on earth as it is in heaven" (Matthew 6:10).

Before the fall, mankind lived in the fullness of the blessing of God on the earth. It was God's desire for His creation to be blessed, and that is why His first decree over mankind was: "And God blessed them" (Genesis 1:28 KJV).

Throughout the Old and New Testaments we see God's full commitment to blessing His people. He blessed Abraham and declared that he would be blessed so that he could be a blessing (Genesis 12:2). We see Him directing His priests to invoke blessing upon the people (Numbers 6:22–26). He called the children of Israel to live in the blessings while journeying with Him in the wilderness (Deuteronomy 28:1–13).

He declared over New Testament believers that they were blessed with every spiritual blessing in the heavenly places and with everything pertaining to life and godliness (Ephesians 1:3; 2 Peter 1:2–4). He truly is a blessing God, and He desires to shower you with blessings so that you will flourish in every area of your life. Jesus came that you would have life in its abundance (John 10:10). Enter the blessing realm and expect blessings to come upon you and overtake you today and all the days of your life.

DECREES

I DECREE THAT:

1. I am created for blessing, and as a result I am overtaken by blessings in every area of my life.

2. I am blessed in the city and blessed in the country. I am blessed coming in and blessed going out.

3. Everything I put my hand to is blessed. My family is blessed. My provision is blessed. All that pertains to me is blessed.

4. I am blessed with victory in every challenge or obstacle I face, for I am the head and not the tail. I am above and not beneath.

5. The Lord has blessed me so that I will be a blessing to others. I cheerfully and bountifully sow blessings into the lives of others, and therefore I reap blessings bountifully.

6. The Lord blesses me and keeps me. He makes His face to shine upon me and is gracious to me. He lifts up His countenance upon me and gives me peace.

7. I am blessed with every spiritual blessing in the heavenly places in Christ, and in Him have been granted everything that pertains to life and godliness.

8. Grace and peace have been multiplied to me, and I have been granted the blessings of all of God's magnificent and glorious promises in Christ Jesus.

9. It is written that what God has blessed no man can curse; therefore, I am blessed in the Lord and cannot be cursed.

10. I am blessed far above all I'm able to ask, think, or imagine!

Decrees based on the following Scriptures: Genesis 1:28; Deuteronomy 28:1–13; Genesis 12:2; 2 Corinthians 9:6–7; Numbers 6:22–26; Ephesians 1:3; 2 Peter 1:2–4; Numbers 23:20; Ephesians 3:20

ACTIVATION

"Count your blessings—name them one by one!" I remember this song from my childhood. It is a good exercise and discipline to thank the Lord each day for the many blessings He has filled your life with. Focus on these wonderful blessings. Make a list of them as you journal today, and give Him praise.

_____

_____

_____

_____

_____

_____

_____

_____

_____

_____

BLESSED WITH FAVOR

For it is You who blesses the righteous man, O LORD,
You surround him with favor as with a shield.

PSALM 5:12

I am sure you have experienced both rejection and favor in your life, and I am confident I can predict which of these two you like better. You were created to experience favor, and that is why rejection is something you naturally attempt to get rid of if it tries to affect your life.

Favor has many benefits. Favor opens doors to opportunities for you. Favor can deliver you from isolation, and favor attracts many blessings to you. In fact, favor is like a blessing magnet, and it is one of God's wonderful gifts freely given to you. He wants you to experience His favor!

Ponder how it might manifest in your life. Imagine yourself walking in absolute favor. For example, you go to work and your coworkers and supervisors are happy to see you. They constantly ask for advice and input because they respect and honor you. The CEO calls you into his or her office and congratulates you on your contribution to the company, and in turn offers you an unexpected promotion and a generous raise.

When you check in for a flight, you are immediately upgraded. When you stand in a long checkout line at your local grocery store, a clerk calls over to you and opens another cash register to accommodate you. The government sends you a letter explaining that they were called to review your taxes over the last seven years and discovered that they owe you money. Included in the letter is a check for thousands of dollars in adjusted taxes. Your relatives adore you and seek your favor. You are dreaming about a certain item you would like, and unexpectedly someone approaches you with a gift— the very item you were dreaming about. You are blessed with many friends, opportunities, gifts, and blessings because favor has filled your life.

These are only some examples of how favor can bless you. This glorious favor is both God's desire for you and His gift to you. Jesus walked in perfect favor, and He has given this favor to everyone who receives Him. It is undeserved, unmerited favor, and it has your name on it!

When you focus on His blessing of favor, you will empower it in your life. You are highly favored in God's eyes, and through faith in His "favor promises" you can live in the fullness of them and experience them every day. With intentionality, daily receive God's blessing of favor by faith and watch it manifest in your life.

DECREES

I DECREE THAT:

1. God's favor in my life is priceless, more valuable than silver or the finest gold.
2. Favor surrounds me like a shield. It covers and protects me from fear and rejection.
3. I am blessed with divine favor that causes my enemies to be at peace with me.
4. God's favor in my life increases positive influence with my family and friends and in my workplace and community.
5. Because of favor in my life, doors of opportunity are opened to me easily.
6. I continue to grow daily in favor and receive favor every place I go.
7. The favor in my life is like a cloud full of spring rain that falls on my life and drenches me like heavenly dew bringing refreshment each day.
8. The Lord favors me. He confirms and establishes that all I put my hands to is blessed.
9. Favor "bathes my feet in butter" and leads my footsteps on the right path.
10. Favor pursues me daily, giving me preferential treatment.

Decrees based on the following Scriptures: Proverbs 22:1; Psalm 5:12; Psalm 30:5, 7; Proverbs 16:17; Luke 2:52; Proverbs 16:15; Proverbs 19:12; Isaiah 45:1; Psalm 45:12; Psalm 90:17; Job 29:6; Psalm 23:6; Job 5:9

ACTIVATION

Make a list of the areas of your life where you do not experience favor, then take time to ponder, dream, and imagine that those areas saturated with God's favor. Pray for your dream to become a reality.

_____

_____

_____

_____

_____

_____

_____

_____

_____

_____

_____

_____

_____

BLESSED WITH FRIENDS

There is a friend who sticks closer than a brother.

PROVERBS 18:24

Can you remember your first friend as a child and how special it was to have someone to share your joy, activities, new toys, and thoughts with? As you grew, you probably acquired more friends and learned about the commitment of friendship.

I am sure that you have had some friends who have been very faithful and loyal to you. These ones are special gifts from God in life. It is God's desire for you to have wonderful friends who you can share your heart, life, and dreams with and who will stand with you in love and faith no matter what. These are true friends. Most people only have one or two of these quality gifts in their lives. They are rare.

I once met a woman who told me she had not had a friend since grade school when her only close classmate betrayed her. I felt so sad that she had not known that special blessing of friendship in her life. She wept, feeling alone and dejected. We prayed and God answered. Within days she had a few people reach out to her, and within a few months she was establishing friendships.

She also came to know the Lord in a personal way during this time and invited Jesus into her heart to be her Savior and Lord. She forgave the one who had betrayed and embarrassed her in childhood. From that point on, she was never friendless again. Jesus became her closest friend and companion. She was amazed at the loved she felt from Him. It was without condition. He lavished her with love each and every day.

Friends are truly a blessing in life, but there is a Friend who trumps all other friends. He is there when your other friends fail and falter, and He is always your greatest support. When we acknowledge Jesus as our primary friend, He will show us how to build good lasting friendships with others. To have good friends, you must *be* a good friend. You will always reap what you sow. With intentionality, sow love and kindness into friendships and you will reap loving and kind friends!

Here are some points to help you cultivate friendships in your life:

- Acknowledge Jesus as your primary friend.
- Thank Him for all the friends you have been blessed with.
- Forgive friends who have not been faithful or loving to you and bless them.
- Pray and ask the Lord for beautiful and powerful friendships.
- Intentionally sow into friendships.

DECREES

I DECREE THAT:

1. Jesus Christ is my primary friend who is closer than a brother. He is a friend of sinners and has drawn me to Himself as His very own.

2. My friend Jesus will not condemn me or judge me. He is always with me.

3. I acquire friends and they love me. They are gifts in my life. I forgive them easily when they make mistakes or fail me. I love my friends that God has gifted me with.

4. By faith, I receive greater grace to be a good friend at all times.

5. My friendships from the past that were destroyed or broken will be restored in perfect love.

6. I am growing stronger, and by faith I decree that new friendships are being strengthened and established in my life.

7. I generously sow love, loyalty, steadfastness, and kindness into others, and therefore I reap friendships that are loving, loyal, steadfast, and kind.

8. I am blessed beyond measure with wonderful life-giving friends in my life.

9. My friends are honorable and always show regard and honor to me and to each other.

10. My friends are not quarrelsome but are very kind, honest, and gentle toward me.

Decrees based on the following Scriptures: Proverbs 18:24; Matthew 11:19; John 8:11; Matthew 7:1; James 4:6; 1 Peter 5:10; 2 Corinthians 9:6; Luke 6:38; Deuteronomy 15:10; 2 Timothy 2:24

ACTIVATION

Make a list of your friends and note how they have blessed you in specific areas of your life. Every friend impacts you differently. Then pray about ways you can sow encouragement and honor into their lives this week.

BLESSED WITH WISDOM

For wisdom is better than jewels;
And all desirable things cannot compare with her.
PROVERBS 8:11

One of my most favorite books in the Bible is the book of Proverbs. It was written by Solomon, who at that time was recognized as the wisest and wealthiest king on the earth. For a number of years, I read the first eight to ten chapters of Proverbs every day because I longed for wisdom and knew that those who meditate on the Word day and night prosper (Psalm 1:1–3). I wanted to be prospered in wisdom!

In the book of Proverbs, I learned some interesting things. For example, wisdom is called the "principal thing" (Proverbs 4:7 KJV). In other words, it is the foundation for many other things in your life. It is very important. You might have knowledge, but if you don't have wisdom, you might not know how to communicate it or apply it. You might have great amounts of money given to you, but if you lack wisdom you could lose it. Wisdom affects every area of your life.

Proverbs also teaches us that if you have wisdom, riches and honor are in her left hand and long life is in her right

(Proverbs 3:16). God spoke to Solomon in a dream and offered him anything he wanted. Solomon asked for wisdom instead of wealth, honor, or the life of his enemies. As a result, God blessed him and said, "I will give you riches and wealth and honor" (2 Chronicles 1:12). What a great choice Solomon made. If he had asked for riches, that would have been all that he received, but because he asked for wisdom, he also received riches, wealth, and honor—in addition victory over his enemies and long life. All those blessings are inside wisdom. When you have wisdom, you have it all!

"Wisdom from above is first pure, then peaceable, gentle, reasonable, full of mercy and goods fruits, unwavering, without hypocrisy" (James 3:17). Would you like to be filled with God's wisdom? You can be. It is a blessing He has for you. Ask in faith and receive.

"But if any of you lacks wisdom, let him ask of God, who gives to all generously and without reproach, and it will be given to him. But he must ask in faith without any doubting" (James 1:5–6).

DECREES

I DECREE THAT:

1. My life is rich with godly wisdom because I love wisdom and search for it with all my heart.

2. I seek wisdom like I would seek silver and hidden treasures.

3. Wisdom is a principle foundation stone in my life, and in every situation I face, I have access to wisdom.

4. I do not lack wisdom; I ask God for it and He generously grants me all I need.

5. I prize and embrace wisdom; therefore, wisdom exalts and honors me.

6. Because I love wisdom, both riches and honor are with me, enduring wealth and righteousness.

7. Wisdom endows me with wealth and fills my treasuries.

8. I walk in the way of wisdom, and therefore I speak noble things. My mouth speaks truth in righteousness when I am empowered by wisdom.

9. Wisdom guards my thoughts, my words, and my ways.

10. I receive wisdom from heaven that is first of all pure, then peace loving, considerate, submissive, full of mercy and good fruit, impartial, and sincere.

Decrees based on the following Scriptures: Ecclesiastes 7:25; Proverbs 2:4; Proverbs 4:6–8; James 1:5; Proverbs 8:17–18; Proverbs 8:21; Proverbs 8:6; Psalm 37:30; Psalm 39:1; James 3:17

ACTIVATION

Pick one situation in your life where you need wisdom. Pray in faith, asking God to make His wise solutions and insights clear to you over the next few days. Be alert, looking for His wisdom. Journal the results.

DAY SEVEN

BLESSED WITH HOPE

"For I know the plans that I have for you," declares the Lord,
"plans for welfare and not for calamity to give
you a future and a hope."

JEREMIAH 29:11

Hope is a joyful expectation for a good outcome. Hope is very powerful, and it is a "launching pad" for your faith to be activated. When faith is activated, it brings forth the manifestation of God's promises in your life. Hope causes good outcomes to break forth. It is a catalyst for breakthroughs in your life and for dreams to come to pass.

Often I hear people say things like, "This is a hopeless situation" or "I feel hopeless." No matter how difficult things might be, we need to always stir up hope and look for ways that we can stir hope in others. God wants to use each of us as His "hope ambassadors." Many times in life we find ourselves in circumstances that attempt to destroy our hope and leave us feeling helpless, low, weak, troubled, and depressed. We never need to give in to the lie of hopelessness because God has promised us "a future and a hope."

Even when situations appear to be the worst they could possibly be, look beyond the problems you face and stir hope in your heart. Cultivate an expectation for something good to happen in spite of your circumstance.

My father has always been a very positive man who has never lost hope. He's faced some serious problems in his life that were challenging for sure. The onlooker, at times, thought it to be impossible for a good outcome to appear, but my father has never looked at how difficult the situation seemed. He has always had hope. When things haven't turned out the way he desired, he has looked beyond the situation and focused on positive things. Even now, as he edges closer to the end of his life, he is still full of hope, joy, fruitfulness, and peace.

God wants to give this promise to those who feel hopeless. May hope come alive within you no matter what you are facing!

"For there is hope for a tree, when it is cut down, that it will sprout again, and its shoots will not fail. Though its roots grow old in the ground and its stump dies in the dry soil, at the scent of water it will flourish and put forth sprigs like a plant" (Job 14:7–9).

DECREES

I DECREE THAT:

1. I am blessed with a bright future that is full of hope and joyful expectation for an awesome outcome.
2. Hope opens up the way and brings breakthroughs in my life, causing my dreams to be realized.
3. I am an ambassador of hope, encouraging others by stirring up hope in their lives.
4. Hope keeps me alive and filled with joy. Hope will never disappoint me or put me to shame.
5. Hope cultivates an expectation in me for good things to happen despite circumstances.
6. Hope in God causes impossibilities in my life to become possibilities.
7. I hope in God and wait with an expectant heart as He answers my prayers.
8. I abound in hope and am filled with joy and peace through the Holy Ghost.
9. Because hope keeps me secure, I can rest in safety and dwell in peace.
10. I am joyful in hope and with patient expectation for all things to work together for good on my behalf.

Decrees based on the following Scriptures: Jeremiah 29:11; Ephesians 1:17–18; 2:10; Proverbs 24:14; Colossians 1:9–10; Jeremiah 17:7; Proverbs 10:28; Psalm 25:2; Romans 5:5–8; Romans 15:13; Romans 12:12; Job 42:2; Jeremiah 32:27; Mark 10:27; Mark 11:24; Romans 15:13; Job 11:18

ACTIVATION

Make note of a circumstance in your life that has caused you to lose hope. Perhaps through the disappointment you faced, your hope for other things in life was lost and you are no longer free to dream. Pray and ask the Lord what He wants you to do to in order to restore your hope.

_____

_____

_____

_____

_____

_____

_____

_____

_____

_____

_____

_____

DAY EIGHT

BLESSED
WITH VICTORY

But thanks be to God, who always leads us in triumph in
Christ, and manifests through us the sweet aroma of the
knowledge of Him in every place.

2 CORINTHIANS 2:14

Did you know that you are a winner and as a winner you
can know victorious outcomes in every battle you face in life?
Life is full of opportunities to overcome—that's right, they are
wonderful opportunities, your "personal resistance training."

I have discovered that it is a positive perspective and a faith-
filled frame of mind that empowers true victories in the midst
of challenging and impossible-looking situations.

David, a young shepherd boy who was inexperienced in
national battles, faced a bully giant (Goliath) who was taunting
God's people, threatening them with what he believed was
imminent defeat. All of Israel was afraid. Goliath was their
"terrorist." No one wanted to face the giant in battle. However,
David had a different perception of this bully than the rest of
Israel. David did not perceive Goliath to be much of anything
and put no stock in his words. In David's perspective he was a

powerless man who had no connection to God or His might whatsoever.

David's perception was in line with God's will, purpose, and might. After all, who was this giant in the light of the greatness of God? God had delivered David and the sheep he was tending whenever the lion and the bear came to attack. As a result of this history with God, David's mind could not understand what the negative and fearful responses from the warriors of Israel were all about. He was up for the battle with full confidence that he would win.

David's mind was set on victory. He had a faith-filled, triumphant frame of mind, and no matter what the giant said, David was set on one thing—slaying the "uncircumcised Philistine" with the power and name of the Lord.

With a positive perception of the situation and a faith-filled frame of mind, David truly did slay the giant with ease, and eventually became king of Israel and went on to win many battles. He prevailed over his enemies. He was victorious!

You can be victorious in all your battles too. With a positive perception of the situation—one that is in line with God's will and purpose—and with faith-filled determination, you will overcome. God will *always* cause you to triumph in every battle. You were created to be a champion!

DECREES

I DECREE THAT:

1. I triumph over my enemies and over all obstacles because God gives me victory over every circumstance.
2. In all things I am more than a conqueror in Christ Jesus.
3. The Lord God goes with me to fight for me against my enemies and gives me the victory.
4. I am thankful to God, who in Christ always leads me into a triumphant procession, rejoicing in victory.
5. I decree that the Lord is full of greatness, power, glory, and majesty, and that He causes me to be victorious!
6. I seek out wise guidance from those who have my best interest at heart, and gain victory in the abundance of wise counselors.
7. I am not afraid. God is with me to deliver me; He is with me to rescue me.
8. I am strong in the Lord and very courageous because God is for me and not against me.
9. My heart is confident and secure in the Lord; though there may be tribulation and trials, I do not fear because He has overcome the world.
10. I proclaim the greatness of God and rejoice in Him because He has won the ultimate and eternal battle for me.

Decrees based on the following Scriptures: 1 Corinthians 15:57; Romans 8:37; Deuteronomy 20:4; 2 Corinthians 2:14; 1 Chronicles 29:11; Proverbs 24:6; Jeremiah 1:8; Romans 8:31; John 16:33; Psalm 18:46–47

ACTIVATION

Define your battle! Are there currently areas of your life where your peace feels threatened? Once you define your battle, identify your fears and apprehensions. Replace them with a victorious perception and faith-filled mind-set.

BLESSED WITH GLADNESS

You have put gladness in my heart,
More than when their grain and new wine abound.

PSALM 4:7

The Lord has blessed you with gladness. The word "gladness" can be defined as a sentiment or condition of welfare and contentment, or the satisfaction that results when your desires are met. How wonderful this is. You are blessed with a sentiment or condition of welfare and contentment, and the elated feelings that come because your desires are met. What a glorious promise from the Lord!

The source of your gladness is not circumstances or people; it is the Lord. Scripture says that He is the one who has put gladness in your heart (Psalm 4:7). Sometimes when circumstances in life are troublesome, you may have to look deep into your heart to find gladness; but it is there, and if you seek you will find.

The apostle Paul is a great example of one who chose to be content in whatever circumstance he found himself in. Look at the following Bible verse and discover how Paul was blessed with welfare and contentment. He chose contentment no matter what he faced. He knew he was blessed by God with gladness, and he received by faith the promise rather than getting depressed over his challenges.

"Therefore I am well content with weaknesses, with insults, with distresses, with persecutions, with difficulties, for Christ's sake; for when I am weak, then I am strong" (2 Corinthians 12:10).

David also knew the secret of living in a state of gladness—the elated feelings that result when your desires are met. He taught us that if we would choose to be glad in the Lord, it would result in the desires of our heart being met. Then when the desires of our heart are met, more gladness is produced.

"Delight yourself in the LORD; and He will give you the desires of your heart" (Psalm 37:4). I have found this to be so true in my own life. When I take time to simply delight in the Lord and put all other thoughts out of my mind, gladness begins to fill me. He is the source of my delight. In the midst of the delight, desires between Him and me mingle and there is always assurance that those desires are met. This in turn increases the gladness of heart.

God wants you to be blessed with gladness of heart. He desires your contentment and fulfillment, and therefore He has blessed you with the promise of gladness.

DECREES

I DECREE THAT:

1. I am filled with gladness because I know that the Lord loves me, no matter what is happening in my life.
2. I am filled with gladness because the Lord causes all things to work together for good in my life.
3. As I delight myself in the Lord, He gives me the desires of my heart and fills me with gladness.
4. My heart is glad because I know that I will dwell in the presence of the Lord forever.
5. You, O Lord, are constantly turning my life from sorrow and disappointment to joy and peace, filling me with gladness.
6. I am overwhelmed with gladness because the Lord provides everything I need. He cares deeply for me.
7. As I trust in the Lord, who is good all the time, I am filled with gladness.
8. As I meditate on the greatness of our God, my heart is glad that I belong to Him.
9. I anticipate the great works of the Lord in my daily life and know that He does not disappoint. This makes me exceedingly glad!
10. As I gladly thank God for His goodness sustaining me in the midst of the trials in my life, Christ is being formed in me.

Decrees based on the following Scriptures: Psalm 16:9; 30:11; 37:4; Romans 8:28; Philippians 4:19

ACTIVATION

Make a list of all the things that you are contented in and also the desires that are already fulfilled in your life. Then thank God for each one. Take note of the increased gladness that will rise up in you as you ponder these things.

_____

_____

_____

_____

_____

_____

_____

_____

_____

_____

_____

BLESSED WITH ABUNDANCE

"The thief comes only to steal and kill and destroy; I came that they may have life, and have it abundantly."

JOHN 10:10

God desires you blessed with a life that is filled with an abundance of every good thing!

Imagine your life filled with an abundance of beautiful friendships and relationships, an abundance of finances, joy, gifting, promotions, favor, wisdom, houses, lands, vehicles, food, and quality clothing to name a few. Does that make your heart glad? It should! The reason it does is because you were created for abundance. God is not a God of lack. He is a God of abundance.

Look at creation. I travel extensively, and everywhere I go, I see God's abundant beauty and provision in all He created both in the heavens and in the earth.

When you look into the sky on a clear night, what do you see? You see an abundance of stars and planets lighting up the sky. It is extravagantly beautiful and causes you to gaze in awe at the greatness of His handiwork.

If you were to stand at the bottom of the Rocky Mountains, what would you see? You would see His abundant majesty in the jagged mountains in all their glory. Yes, you would stand in awe of Him!

Stand at the seashore of one of His great oceans and gaze all the way to the horizon. Is there the revelation of abundance in what you see?

What about in desert lands? Look at the sand and the open sky. When I once went on an Arabian Desert excursion, I was speechless when I saw the endless miles of desert with the sun glistening upon the sand and the blue sky above it all proclaiming God's extravagant greatness.

God is a God of abundance, and He has blessed you with many promises of abundance. You were not created for lack. You were created in His image and likeness. Expect His abundant goodness and it will be attracted to you. You were created for it—for Him. Receive His blessing of abundance by faith.

DECREES

I DECREE THAT:

1. Jesus came to give me abundant life. I have an abundance of friends and family, wisdom, power, provision, love, and every good thing.

2. God gives me abundantly of the earth, its grain and new wine.

3. When the earth experiences famine, I will always have abundance.

4. God is blessing me abundantly, so that in all things, at all times, I have all that I need and am able to do every good work that He has planned for me.

5. I feast on the abundance of the house of the Lord, and He gives me drink from the river of His delights.

6. God will reveal Himself to me in ways that are exceedingly abundantly above all that I can ask or think.

7. The Lord will lavish me with good things. He will open up the treasure vaults of heaven and bless all the work of my hands.

8. As I seek the Lord, I shall lack no good thing; He abundantly supplies me with all that I need.

9. The Lord causes me to increase and abound in abundant love for the people He brings across my path.

10. As I am filled with His joy and peace, I receive abundance of hope, by the power of the Holy Spirit.

Decrees based on the following Scriptures: John 10:10; Genesis 27:28; Psalm 37:19; Luke 6:38; 2 Corinthians 9:8; Psalm 36:8; 84:11; Deuteronomy 28:12; 1 Thessalonians 3:12; Romans 15:13

ACTIVATION

Take note of areas in your life that are not in the category of abundance at this time. Worship God as the God of abundance over those areas with living faith and passion, and watch for what God will do.

BLESSED WITH MARRIAGE

For this reason a man shall leave his father and mother and shall be joined to his wife, and the two shall become one flesh. This mystery is great; but I am speaking with reference to Christ and the church.

EPHESIANS 5:31–32

Marriage represents a profound love mystery—Christ and the church. In the very beginning of the Bible, we discover that God created man (male and female) in His image and likeness and then blessed them together to be fruitful, to multiply, to fill the earth and rule over it (Genesis 1:27–28).

God is Love. Mankind was created in the image and the likeness of Love. When a man and a woman commit to God's Love in a marriage covenant, then we see blessing, multiplication, and dominion manifest.

The marriage union between a man and his wife is intended to display a model of Christ's covenant love and union with His church. It is no wonder that marriage is often under attack. The potential of a love-filled marriage union is enormous, not only for personal life blessings for the couple but also for the manifest dominion of Christ and His heavenly kingdom in the earth.

There are five main attacks we see in the war against marriage today:

- Hindering of those who desire to be married from finding their right mate and committing to the marriage covenant.
- Broken marriage covenants due to love failures and violations of the covenant.
- Keeping couples from understanding the fullness of their marriage potential as God designed it.
- Premature death of a spouse.
- Confusion as to the definition of marriage as outlined in the Scriptures (one man and one woman covenanted together as man and wife).

Marriage is worth fighting for. Jesus taught us that the thief comes to steal, kill, and destroy (John 10:10), so we know there is a very real enemy against marriage. However, God has given us victorious and powerful weapons to use in this battle.

"For though we walk in the flesh, we do not war according to the flesh, for the weapons of our warfare are not of the flesh, but divinely powerful for the destruction of fortresses. We are destroying speculations and every lofty thing raised up against the knowledge of God, and we are taking every thought captive to the obedience of Christ" (2 Corinthians 10:3–5).

Rise up and fight the battle for godly marriages with your love and faith.

DECREES

I DECREE THAT:

1. My spouse and I are one flesh and are walking in unity together by the power of God's Holy Spirit. We live under the His blessing.

2. My marriage is a picture of the mystery of Christ and the church, and it is rooted and grounded in the Lord's unfailing love.

3. I walk in love toward my spouse and as such do not take into account a wrong suffered and keep no record of wrongs. I am patient with my spouse, hoping all things and believing all things.

4. Just as the Lord has forgiven me every sin, I also forgive continuously, bearing with my spouse, putting on a heart of compassion and kindness.

5. The blood of Jesus covers my spouse, me, and my marriage. My marriage is centered on God and is thriving.

6. Clear communication is flowing, and the Holy Spirit is imparting God-given understanding for one another to both of us.

7. What God has joined together, no one will break apart.

8. The Lord's plan for my marriage is to prosper it and to give my spouse and me a hope and a future. I love and serve my spouse in the strength of the Lord.

9. I am destroying the lies of the enemy by taking every thought captive to the obedience of Christ. I believe the Lord's promises for my marriage.

10. No word or curse spoken against my marriage shall have effect. Only the blessing of the Lord will cover my marriage.

Decrees based on the following Scriptures: Ephesians 4:32; 5:31–32; 1 Corinthians 10:5; 13:4–7; Psalm 133; Mark 10:9; Galatians 5:13; Colossians 3:13; Proverbs 26:2; Jeremiah 29:11

ACTIVATION

Two powerful weapons to empower marriages are:

1. Prayer. When you make intentional, focused requests of God in pure faith according to His will for marriage quality, He hears you and grants your desire (1 John 5:14–15).

2. Decrees. When you proclaim the promises of God in faith and determination into marriage, His Word goes forth to accomplish itself. It does not return void but brings itself to pass (Isaiah 55:10–11).

Write out prayers for your marriage and bring them before the Lord in faith. Make daily decrees of His Word for your marriage.

BLESSED WITH FAMILY

Ascribe to the LORD, O families of the peoples,
Ascribe to the LORD glory and strength.

PSALMS 96:7

On a recent trip to Israel, I was blessed to see families coming together to celebrate the Sabbath. My Jewish friends explained that the Sabbath is extremely important for the strength and unity of the family. Every week they traditionally gather on the Sabbath to spend time together. Those who work in a different community, are away at school, or serve in the military will travel home each week to meet with the family whenever possible. They share a special dinner, prayer, reading of the Scriptures, and fellowship, and then the father blesses his wife, children, and household. It is a time when they focus on God and family together. What a great investment!

I remember, as a child growing up in Canada, Sunday being a national day of rest. I did not grow up in a Christian family, but the whole nation, whether Christian or not, observed Sunday as a day when no stores or businesses were open—only emergency services. Many attended church services, and families traditionally shared a special Sunday meal and fellowship time together.

I recall the very day when the government passed the law allowing stores and services to be open on Sundays. Everyone was so happy for this newfound freedom, but I find it interesting that since that time, the family has become more fragmented. Rarely do most families share meals together or prayer and worship experiences at the "family altar." Everyone is so busy, and the family has suffered.

It is time for focus on the family to return. The family is the most important relational unit in society. When the family is strong, communities and nations will be strong and blessings will follow.

Oh, that families would return to the Lord, and together love and worship Him and love each other. When investment is made into building family, the returns will impact nations.

Let's believe together for a powerful outpouring of the Spirit upon home and family in this hour. Let's believe for love and honor for God and each other to fill every home.

DECREES

I DECREE THAT:

1. My family is walking in the light of God's love, and all dark schemes of the enemy will be utterly thwarted.

2. There is no lack in my family, because God provides for our every spiritual, emotional, physical, social, and financial need according to His riches in glory.

3. A wall of God's fire of protection surrounds my family.

4. My home is a sanctuary of peace and love for my family, and we dwell together in safety.

5. Every member of my family is full of joy and faith, trusting in the Lord.

6. All my children and grandchildren are taught of the Lord and have an intimate relationship with Him. Great is their peace.

7. My family is strong, and we love one another with the love of the Lord.

8. My family will walk in all the works God has prepared for us from before the foundation of the world.

9. Our family dwells together in unity, and our relationships with one another are good and pleasant.

10. Grace and favor rest upon our family.

Decrees based on the following Scriptures: Psalms 1:3; 4:8; 90:16–17; 125:2; 133:1; Proverbs 10:22; Isaiah 54:13–14, 17; Zechariah 2:5; Ephesians 2:10

ACTIVATION

Make a list of the blessings you see in your family, and pray for ways that you can invest in building relationships in your home and family.

DAY THIRTEEN

BLESSED WITH ENDURANCE

Let us run with endurance the race that is set before us, fixing our eyes on Jesus, the author and perfecter of faith, who for the joy set before Him endured the cross, despising the shame, and has sat down at the right hand of the throne of God.

HEBREWS 12:1B–2

Jesus endured maltreatment, betrayal, abandonment, slander, humiliation, and cruelty during His life and ministry in the earth. The word "endurance" (*hupomone* in Greek) has several meanings, including persistence, patience, commitment, and dedication. Jesus' focus on the outcome—His prize—was His motivation to endure. "For the *joy* set before Him, He endured…" You are the *joy* that was set before Him. You are His prize.

A friend of mine was a popular athlete in college, and he shared with me that before he ran a race, he walked past the trophies that were to be presented to the winners. He stood and gazed upon the gold, silver, and bronze trophies that were displayed. The prize was his motivation to endure in the race. He always kept his mind on the prize as he ran.

Focusing on the glorious outcome is a great motivator in life. Whenever you lose sight of the prize, you can become vulnerable to discouragement in the journey.

For years I was a strong starter but a poor finisher. I was highly motivated to plunge into something new, but I became bored or discouraged during the journey and as a result often failed to complete many projects.

One day, the Lord spoke to my heart and said, "Winners never quit and quitters never win. You have need of endurance." Those words pierced my heart, and I made a serious inner resolve to be a strong finisher. God's grace breathed upon that resolve, and to this day I am both a great starter and a strong finisher.

Jesus is the true champion when it comes to endurance. You need not strive within yourself to embrace endurance. Jesus has blessed you with His ability to endure when you position yourself to receive it by faith. When I lack endurance, I humble myself before the Lord and ask Him to fill me with the grace to endure—and He does.

His blessing of endurance is available to you also, whenever you need it.

DECREES

I DECREE THAT:

1. Jesus Christ fills me with grace to endure.
2. I behold the joy set before me.
3. Discouragement flees from me because God grants me endurance and encouragement.
4. I lay aside the weights that easily ensnare me and keep me from finishing strong.
5. I am a strong finisher.
6. Jesus is the author and the finisher of my faith.
7. The testing of my faith produces endurance so that I am complete, lacking nothing.
8. I run with endurance the race set before me.
9. Rewards of endurance constantly bless my life.
10. As I am encouraged with endurance, I freely encourage others to endure.

Decrees based on the following Scriptures: Hebrews 12:1–2; Romans 15:5; James 1:3–4; James 5:11; Hebrews 11:6; Matthew 10:8

ACTIVATION

Take note of an area (or areas) in your life where you have need of endurance. Invite the Lord to empower you with His endurance in that area (or those areas). Determine to press through when you feel like quitting.

_____

_____

_____

_____

_____

_____

_____

_____

_____

_____

_____

BLESSED WITH GOD'S PRESENCE

And He said, "My presence shall go with you,
and I will give you rest."

EXODUS 33:14

The first time I felt the tangible presence of the Lord was the night I surrendered my life to Jesus Christ. The presence of His love was so heavy that evening as He gloriously dissolved my sin, fears, guilt, and shame.

Over the years I grew in the Lord and was blessed to experience other aspects of His presence: His holiness, power, and glory. God loves to manifest Himself to us. It is the privilege of every believer to encounter His tangible presence, but it is important to know that whether we feel His presence or not, He is always with us.

My grandson called me one day and said, "Grandma, did you know that just because you can't see something doesn't mean it's not real?" What a beautiful insight he received. He was learning at a young age how to believe the truth about God and His kingdom whether you encounter it in the natural or not.

God promises that He will never leave us or forsake us. That means His presence is always with us. When we receive Him into our heart as our personal Savior, He enters our lives and abides in us. He is always in us even when we do not feel Him. Here are three keys to help you experience God's presence in your life:

1. *Believe* in His presence that is already with you, in you, and around you. His presence goes before you. Do you believe this? It is vital to have faith in His promises concerning His presence with you.

2. *Look for His presence.* Exercise an intentional awareness of His presence in all that you do and everywhere you go. What you focus on, you will empower. If you seek, you will find.

3. *Worship Him.* Worship causes your focus to be upon Him and upon Him alone. An atmosphere of true worship is an atmosphere of divine presence. Sometimes I like to listen to worship music for hours. Oh, the Lord's presence becomes so strong.

God's presence is with you—always.

DECREES

I DECREE THAT:

1. God's presence goes with me everywhere I am, and He gives me rest.
2. Because I choose to abide in love, I abide in God and His presence is with me.
3. In His presence there is fullness of joy. I overflow with joy as I abide in His presence, and at His right hand I have pleasures forevermore.
4. As I dwell in His presence, He keeps me from all harm.
5. I love spending time in God's presence, basking in His Love and returning my love to Him.
6. My enemies must flee from before me seven ways at the presence of the Lord. The mountains bow and the hills melt like wax.
7. My heart is glad and my spirit rejoices because God dwells with the contrite and lowly of spirit in order to revive the spirit of the lowly and to revive the heart of the contrite.
8. I experience the tangible presence of the Lord as I worship the Lord with praise and thanksgiving.
9. God's presence fills the atmosphere of my life as I go about doing good.
10. My family, my house, and all that belongs to me is secure as I'm aware of the presence of God in my life.

Decrees based on the following Scriptures: Exodus 33:14; 1 John 4:16; Psalm 16:11; Psalm 91; Psalm 95:2; Deuteronomy 28:7; Psalm 97:5; Isaiah 57:15; James 4:8; Acts 10:38; Psalm 16

ACTIVATION

Take some time to worship the Lord and acknowledge the presence of God in you and around you. Journal what you sense. Respond to God with love and adoration.

BLESSED WITH GLORY

"The glory which You have given Me I have given to them."

JOHN 17:22

The word *glory*, found in the Bible in both Old Testament Hebrew and New Testament Greek, is a powerful word and refers to a number of qualities pertaining to God. It can mean splendor, brightness, magnificence, an exalted state, abundance, majesty, praise, weight, preeminence, dignity, grace, wealth, and riches.

These qualities are in Christ. All glory has been given to Him, and He has in turn given this glory to you. That means you are already blessed with all these wonderful attributes. Christ's presence in you *is* the glory of God, and by faith you can be filled to overflowing with all the aspects of it. The Bible discloses that, "the earth will be filled with the knowledge of the glory of the Lord, as the waters cover the sea" (Habakkuk 2:14).

How will this happen? It will come to pass as a result of the outpouring of the glory through God's people, who let it pour forth out of their lives to reach the world around them!

In 2 Chronicles 5:13–14 we find the priests worshiping the

Lord in unity, proclaiming the goodness of God: "In unison when the trumpeters and the singers were to make themselves heard with one voice to praise and to glorify the LORD ... and when they praised the LORD saying, *'He indeed is good for His lovingkindness is everlasting,'* then the house, the house of the LORD, was filled with a cloud, so that the priests could not stand to minister because of the cloud, for the glory of the LORD filled the house of God."

What I have discovered is that when I worship the Lord and take time to meditate on and declare His goodness and lovingkindness/mercy (not His wrath or anger), then the presence of His glory falls and activates. How beautiful is the way the Lord has extravagantly blessed us with His glory.

In Moses' tabernacle, the glory hovered over the mercy seat (not the judgment seat, see Exodus 25:17–22) and God would speak to His people concerning His will and purpose for the nation from that place. Acknowledging and decreeing His goodness and mercy is the key for experiencing His glory.

Through God's great kindness and mercy, you have been blessed with His glory. What an extravagant gift of love!

DECREES

I DECREE THAT:

1. God gave me the same glory given to Jesus.
2. The spirit of wisdom and revelation in the knowledge of knowing Him intimately is what I possess in His glory.
3. Because the earth shall be filled with the knowledge of the glory of the Lord, as the waters cover the sea, I am expressing His glory everywhere I go.
4. I reflect Jesus Christ, who is the brightness of the glory of God.
5. I walk in integrity and good moral standing before God and man because I am crowned with glory and with honor.
6. God created me for His glory. He formed me and made me in His image of glory; therefore, I shine His light and love.
7. I am fruitful in my life, bearing good fruit always, because of the glory that is activated within me.
8. Prosperity and health are mine as glory follows me and precedes me.
9. I am being strengthened daily with power in my innermost being as I meditate on the riches of His glory.
10. I am successful in all I put my hands to. The Lord perfects everything concerning me as He fills me with His glory.

Decrees based on the following Scriptures: John 17:22; Ephesians 1:17–21; Habakkuk 2:14; Hebrews 1:3; Isaiah 43:7; Psalm 8:5; John 15:8; Isaiah 58:8; Isaiah 52:12; Ephesians 3:16; Psalm 133:8

ACTIVATION

Journal everything that comes to your mind concerning the goodness and mercy God has shown you. Then meditate on these things, thanking Him for each one. Speak them aloud and take note of any sense of His glory manifestations you encounter over the next week.

_____

_____

_____

_____

_____

_____

_____

_____

_____

_____

_____

DAY SIXTEEN

BLESSED WITH FINANCIAL PROSPERITY

"The silver is Mine and the gold is Mine,"
declares the LORD of hosts.

HAGGAI 2:8

Many have been deceived into thinking that living in financial poverty is holy and pleasing to God. I have ministered for many years on mission fields in developing nations, and I can assure you that there is absolutely nothing holy at all about poverty. Where the spirit of poverty hovers, you will find discouragement, depression, sickness, uncleanness, clutter, lawlessness, corruption, lack of stewardship of belongings and property, fear, and bondage. It is gross, and as believers we should not partake of it.

When my husband and I first started in full-time preaching ministry, the Lord invited us to live by faith with no visible means of support. We were to tell no one of our needs—only Him. For five years we daily stood on the promises of God's Word for provision. It was a very challenging period, and we were tempted daily with lies in our mind that taunted, "You are on the wrong path. God is not providing and He won't. You are deceived to think He will."

It appeared that lack was prevailing, rather than the abundant life that was promised, but we faithfully stood on the Word regarding His provision.

The Bible says that you will reap in "due time" if you do not grow weary in well doing (Galatians 6:9). Believing God's Word and obeying it is "well doing," so we trusted that in God's appointed time we would reap. Sometimes it feels like the Word is not working, but if you prevail standing in faith, your "due time" will come.

Our breakthrough came very suddenly after five years of prevailing with His promises, and we are still living in the amazing breakthrough today. I have been both rich and poor—and I like rich better. It gives God glory when we live out His will on the earth as it is in heaven.

God wants you blessed not only with financial provision but also with the wisdom to steward it. The Bible teaches that when you are faithful with unrighteous mammon (money), you can then be trusted with true riches (Luke 16:11).

May you experience abundance in financial provision and walk in His wisdom to steward it well. It is His will for you.

DECREES

I DECREE THAT:

1. All the gold and all the silver belongs to God. Because I am His child, I have access to all that is His through Jesus.
2. My God meets all my needs according to His riches in glory by Christ.
3. I look to God as the source of all my provision.
4. I worship and love God and not money.
5. God gives me my daily bread (needs and requirements).
6. All the good things I need and enjoy in life follow me as I follow the Lord.
7. The Lord makes me abound in prosperity.
8. Financial blessings come upon me and overtake me.
9. I will lend to many but shall not borrow.
10. I increase and multiply in houses, land, gold, and silver, and when I do, I will not forget the Lord my God. I will worship Him, follow Him, and obey Him all the days of my life.

Decrees based on the following Scriptures: Haggai 2:8; Philippians 4:19; Matthew 6:4; Matthew 6:11; Psalm 23:6; Deuteronomy 28:2, 11–12; Deuteronomy 8:11–13, 18

ACTIVATION

Journal a number of Bible promises concerning God's provision for your life and meditate on them daily. Allow God to speak to you with encouraging thoughts concerning your finances. Journal what you believe He is speaking to you. Worship Him as the wonderful provider of all your financial needs.

_____

_____

_____

_____

_____

_____

_____

_____

_____

_____

BLESSED WITH THE HOLY SPIRIT

"But the Helper, the Holy Spirit, whom the Father will send in My name, He will teach you all things, and bring to your remembrance all that I said to you."

JOHN 14:26

The Holy Spirit is not a mere influence or power; He is the spirit of God Himself who has been given as the Father's gift to those who believe in Christ. He is God's presence and being with you—in you. The Holy Spirit is the very spirit of Christ.

John 3 tells the story when Jesus talked with Nicodemus, a religious man who was inquiring about the kingdom of God. Jesus explained to him that in order to enter the kingdom, he must be born again. Nicodemus tried to process that comment with his own mind but couldn't grasp it. Jesus further explained to him, "That which is born of the Spirit is spirit" (John 3:6). In other words, the Holy Spirit will enter into the spirit of those who invite Christ to be their Savior, and give them entrance into the kingdom of God.

Man (male and female) is a three-part being: spirit, soul, and body. Rebirth takes place when the Spirit of God enters man's spirit. A miracle occurs and the individual becomes a brand-new creation within (2 Corinthians 5:17).

The Holy Spirit is in every believer to lead, guide, teach, empower, convict, and direct. What a gift! Jesus said, "He who believes in Me, as the Scripture said, 'From his innermost being will flow rivers of living water.' But this He spoke of the Spirit, whom those who believed in Him were to receive" (John 7:38–39). That means we can open our hearts to release His power and love to the world around us. In Acts 1:8, Jesus taught the disciples that not only could the Holy Spirit dwell within but He could also rest upon us. We shall also be "baptized with the Holy Spirit" (fully immersed in Him), according to Acts 1:5.

God so passionately desires to dwell with His people that He has fully given Himself to be in us and on us, and to completely fill us.

If we yield ourselves to Him, inviting His Spirit to come into our life, He will come. The more you yield, the more He fills. Invite Him to fill you afresh right now. Receive His presence and empowerment by faith.

DECREES

I DECREE THAT:

1. The Holy Spirit lives mightily within me and has given me new life in the kingdom of God through Jesus Christ.

2. The Holy Spirit teaches me all things and reveals Christ to me.

3. The Holy Spirit leads and guides me into all truth.

4. I am filled with and empowered by the sovereign Spirit of the Lord, wisdom, understanding, counsel, strength, knowledge, and the fear of the Lord.

5. The same spirit that raised Christ from the dead dwells within me and brings life, strength, and health to my mortal body.

6. I have a life-giving communion and relationship with God through the Holy Spirit.

7. I am bold to testify of the goodness and truth of God because of the Holy Spirit's empowerment in my life.

8. The Holy Spirit convicts me of sin, righteousness, and judgment.

9. I have insights for the future through the Holy Spirit.

10. The Holy Spirit discloses to me what belongs to me in Jesus Christ.

Decrees based on the following Scriptures: John 3:3–6; John 14:26; Isaiah 11:2; Ephesians 3:20; Romans 8:11; 2 Corinthians 13:14; Acts 1:8; John 16:8–15

ACTIVATION

Take some time to be quiet in the presence of God and invite His Spirit to come and fill you afresh. Soak in His love and meditate on His presence that dwells in you and that is upon you. By faith, drink of His goodness. Journal your experience and any insight He gives you.

BLESSED WITH POWER

"But you will receive power when the Holy Spirit has come upon you."

ACTS 1:8

The word "power" in most New Testament passages is translated from the Greek word *dynamis*. A few of the usages of this word in the Bible are:

- Might, power, and aptitude.
- Authority for performing miracles.
- A state of moral excellence.
- The influence and authority that result from affluence.

The Holy Spirit has given you access to dynamis and all the benefits listed above, and you can activate it by faith.

When you are feeling weak and lacking in might or aptitude, receive dynamis by faith and you will be strengthened and empowered. Numerous times when I have felt tired or weak, I have invited the Holy Spirit through a simple prayer to empower and refresh me, and immediately I have been energized. This is dynamis power at work.

A number of years ago, the Holy Spirit spoke to me, saying, "I want you to write a book for Me." I responded, "But Lord, I am not an author." He answered, "But I am. I authored the Scriptures, and I will give you the power to write for Me." That day, by faith, I received the aptitude to write books. He gave me the dynamis—the aptitude—and I have been authoring books ever since.

Dynamis also gives you the authority to work miracles. A woman came for prayer one day as she was barren. I prayed in faith, and dynamis power released the miracle. Within a year, I received a photo of her beautiful baby boy. God is powerful and His dynamis can flow through you.

Another aspect of dynamis is moral excellence. By faith you can receive dynamis to fortify your soul, bringing it into a state of moral excellence. I love integrity, truth, and righteous morals. Dynamis produces these things in our lives.

Dynamis also gives you the power to create affluence and to influence the world through the abundance you receive.

You have been blessed with God's power. As a believer, His dynamis resides within you. Activate it by faith.

"Now to Him who is able to do far more abundantly beyond all that we ask or think, according to the power that works within us" (Ephesians 3:20).

DECREES

I DECREE THAT:

1. God's power dwells within me by His Spirit.
2. God's power is upon my life and activated to bless the world around me.
3. I have moral excellence due to God's power living within me.
4. I have the authority to work miracles in Christ as I activate them through faith and obedience to the Spirit.
5. I can do all things through Christ who enables me.
6. I have the power to obtain wealth.
7. The sick are healed by the power of Christ when I lay hands on them.
8. In Christ's power and name, I cast out demons.
9. Through Christ, I have power over all the power of the enemy and nothing will injure me.
10. I preach the gospel boldly through the power of the Spirit.

Decrees based on the following Scriptures: Acts 1:5, 8; Philippians 4:13; Deuteronomy 8:18; Mark 16:17–18; Luke 10:19

ACTIVATION

Make a list of areas of your life where you would like to see dynamis activated, and then pray in faith to release God's power into those areas. Take steps of faith to activate His power (for example, if you know someone who is sick, lay hands on that person believing for healing). Journal your prayers and actions, and record the results.

BLESSED WITH THE GIFTS OF THE HOLY SPIRIT

Pursue love, yet desire earnestly spiritual gifts.

1 CORINTHIANS 14:1

In my early twenties I came to Christ, and very soon afterward I received powerful teaching on the gifts of the Holy Spirit. As a result, I have lived in a culture of Holy Spirit activation my entire life in the Lord.

As we read through the gospels in the New Testament, we find Jesus healing the sick, casting out demons, raising the dead, cleansing lepers, releasing words of knowledge and wisdom, and prophesying all throughout His ministry on earth. He then declares in John 14:12, "Truly, truly, I say to you, he who believes in Me, the works that I do, he will do also; and greater works than these shall he do because I go to the Father."

Normal Christianity does not begin or end with church attendance but rather is marked by believers doing the works of Jesus in His love and faith. So often we settle for a gospel without power, which in reality is not the gospel at all. Demonstrations of power, miracles, signs, and wonders accompanied Jesus, and they are to follow all believers.

Mark 16:15 commissions us to preach the gospel to every creature, but it further instructs in verse 17 and 18 that signs will follow those who believe: "In My name they will cast out demons, they will speak with new tongues; they will pick up serpents, and if they drink any deadly poison, it will not hurt them; they will lay hands on the sick, and they will recover."

Jesus wants us to be fully endowed with the gifts of the Spirit so that we can do the same works He did. You cannot earn gifts; they are given. You simply need to receive. The gifts of the Spirit are received by faith, and by faith we activate them.

Paul gave Timothy a warning about the end times. He revealed that there would be a people holding to a form of godliness but denying the power (2 Timothy 3:5). We are not to deny His gifts that demonstrate His power and presence.

Let's be a people who fully function in His amazing gifts. They are available to all believers in the Holy Spirit.

DECREES

I DECREE THAT:

1. All the gifts of the Spirit dwell within me and can be activated through me.
2. I am able to speak with new tongues and edify myself in the Lord.
3. I have the supernatural ability to interpret tongues.
4. I can prophesy and encourage people through speaking God's destiny words for them.
5. I am empowered with the gift of wisdom.
6. I host the gift of the word of knowledge and can know God's mysteries and things about people and circumstances that only God can reveal.
7. The gift of the discerning of spirits dwells within me, giving me the ability to discern the presence and specific identity of God, His angels, the spirit of natural man, the devil, and his demons.
8. I function in the gift of faith, which enables me to connect into the supernatural empowerment of God. Gifts of healings flow through me to the sick and infirm.
9. The gift of the performing of miracles is functioning in me for the working of various types of miracles.

Decrees based on the following Scriptures: 1 Corinthians 12:4–7

ACTIVATION

Remember some of the times you have prayed for God to move in His gifts through you. If you have not experienced being used in this way yet, craft a prayer and write it in your journal, asking God to teach you and use you to demonstrate His love through the power of His gifts. There are great teachings on this subject in the body of Christ that you can access to help in your growth. Pursue teaching and instruction—and then activate.

BLESSED WITH THE MIND OF CHRIST

For who has known the mind of the Lord,
that he will instruct him?
But we have the mind of Christ.

1 CORINTHIANS 2:16

Have you ever thought of how wonderful it would be to think just like God? I have good news for you: you can. When the Spirit of God dwells within you, you have the mind of Christ. It is given to you in your salvation package when you receive Christ. Very few, however, activate and utilize it, but every believer can.

How many times have you leaned on your own understanding for solutions to problems before going to the Lord for His divine answers? I believe we all fall short in this, but we can change our ways and seek Him for insight, solutions, knowledge, wisdom, counsel, and understanding whenever we are in need of these things. All these blessings are available to us in the mind of Christ, all the time. We simply need to access His mind by faith.

Here are some keys to help you cultivate the activation of the mind of Christ that dwells within you:

- Believe that you possess the mind of Christ within your new nature.
- Nurture the mind of Christ within you by the renewing of your mind through the Word. Meditate on His Word and you will discern the will and ways of God.
- When needing insights, solutions, knowledge, wisdom, counsel, and understanding for situations in life, inquire of the Lord by humbling yourself before Him and requesting His response through prayer.
- Spend time with the Lord, listening for Him to share His heart with you and waiting on Him with expectation for His divine insights.
- When you receive His insights, believe them and apply them.

Bible characters like Daniel and Joseph had "divine intelligence" operating in their lives. They knew God's solutions for problems and as a result they affected their nation. Can you imagine what the world would be like if every Christian accessed the mind of Christ? I think the world would be a better place. Don't you?

DECREES

I DECREE THAT:

1. I have the mind of Christ residing in my inner man.
2. The mind of Christ lives big in me and is full of all the knowledge, wisdom, insights, understanding, and solutions that I need.
3. I possess "divine intelligence."
4. I do not lean unto my own understanding but in all my ways acknowledge God.
5. God's ways are higher than my way; therefore I humble myself before Him and receive His understanding.
6. Through the mind of Christ I can access the knowledge of witty inventions.
7. The mind of Christ reveals things I need to know about the future.
8. The mind of Christ teaches me to make godly decisions daily.
9. The mind of Christ grants me good memory and recall.
10. I have the ability to retain knowledge.

Decrees based on the following Scriptures: 1 Corinthians 2:16; Daniel 1:4; Proverbs 3:5–6; Isaiah 55:9; Proverbs 8:12; John 16:13; Proverbs 10:7

ACTIVATION

Identify some situations in your life at this time that you do not have answers for or that you would welcome God's thoughts and insights into. Write them down and then inquire of the Lord. Wait for Him to speak and then write down any insights you receive.

Praise and thank the Lord every day that you have His mind living within you. What you focus on, you empower.

DAY TWENTY-ONE

BLESSED
WITH COURAGE

Be strong and let your heart take courage,
all you who hope in the LORD.

PSALM 31:24

Many situations in life can create reactions of fear and intimidation. I think of Joshua for example, leading Israel into the Promised Land after Moses died. Look at what God said to Joshua in chapter 1:6–7, 9:

"*Be strong and courageous,* for you shall give this people possession of the land which I swore to their fathers to give them.

"*Only be strong and very courageous;* be careful to do according to all the law which Moses My servant commanded you; do not turn from it to the right or to the left, so that you may have success wherever you go.

"Have I not commanded you? *Be strong and courageous!* Do not tremble or be dismayed, for the LORD your God is with you wherever you go."

God understood that the assignment He was giving Joshua was greater than Joshua's experience or human ability. That is why he needed courage.

In short, courage is the ability or strength to face difficulties and fears. It is not the absence of them. It took great courage for Jesus to go to the cross. It took courage for Elijah to confront the prophets of Baal. It took courage for Paul to go into regions that were hostile to the gospel. It took courage for Esther to go before the king. All of these individuals faced difficult situations and overcame fear with an attribute of God called courage.

You have the God-given blessing of courage living in you. When you feel intimidated, overwhelmed, or fearful in life, you can draw on the courage God has given you within. When you ask God to give you courage, you will feel strength, confidence, and boldness rise within your inner self. This blessing of courage can be received by faith. The next time you face a difficult situation, you can remember to draw on God-given courage.

My son was bullied in school when he was younger, and he desired to quit school as a result. We had a meeting with the counselor, who shared with him about the power of courage—the ability to face his fears. He chose to go the way of an overcomer and gloriously overcame by praying for courage each day before he went to school. That year became the most character-building year of all. He finished strong and gained popularity that year.

Courage is a powerful attribute that you have in Christ. Be courageous!

DECREES

I DECREE THAT:

1. I have been blessed with a courageous heart.
2. My heart fully trusts in the Lord because it is He who restores hope and gives me strength to go the distance.
3. I abound in the work of the Lord and am steadfast and immovable in Him.
4. I encourage myself with positive words and with the Scriptures. King David encouraged himself in the Lord.
5. I am strong and courageous, and I encourage those surrounding me to be strong and courageous.
6. I lean daily on God's understanding, and He strengthens me and gives me wisdom and knowledge.
7. My heart is steadfast and fixed, and I do not fear when trouble comes.
8. I am bold and courageous because the Lord is always with me. He never leaves me or forsakes me.
9. The Lord grants me strength and boldness to endure.
10. Daily I am encouraged as I meditate on the life-giving Word of God.

Decrees based on the following Scriptures: Psalm 31:24;
1 Corinthians 16:13; Psalm 27:14; Proverbs 3:5–6; Mark 5:36;
Psalm 112:7; Psalm 112:8; Psalm 19:14; Joshua 1:6; Psalm 105:4;
Psalm 1:1–3

ACTIVATION

Make a list of situations in your life that cause you to feel afraid or intimidated. Go through each one and imagine yourself being full of courage and overcoming. What does that look like to you?

If you have a current situation where you are facing difficulties, pray for courage and then activate your courage.

_____

_____

_____

_____

_____

_____

_____

_____

_____

_____

DAY TWENTY-TWO

BLESSED WITH HEALTH AND HEALING

Bless the LORD, O my soul,
And forget none of His benefits;
Who pardons all your iniquities,
Who heals all your diseases.

PSALM 103:2–3

God desires His people to live in perfect health. In heaven there is no sickness or disease, and God longs for you to experience heaven's reality while living on the earth.

In the beginning of creation, there was no sickness or disease—it came into the earth through the sin of mankind. Sin corrupts, and whenever we sow to the flesh, we reap corruption. But God had a redemptive plan even in the Old Testament and introduced Himself to His people as their Healer.

And He said, "If you will give earnest heed to the voice of the LORD your God, and do what is right in His sight, and give ear to His commandments, and keep all His statutes, I will put none of the diseases on you which I have put on the Egyptians; for I, the LORD, am your Healer" (Exodus 15:26).

God further demonstrated His mercy and kindness to us by sending His Son, Jesus, to heal the sick and infirm.

"Surely our griefs He Himself bore, and our sorrows He carried; yet we ourselves esteemed Him stricken, smitten of God, and afflicted. But He was pierced through for our transgressions, He was crushed for our iniquities; *the chastening for our well-being fell upon Him, and by His scourging we are healed*" (Isaiah 53:4–5).

All through the New Testament we see Jesus healing all who came to Him for healing from every manner of sickness and disease, and in the book of Acts we see believers doing the same works Jesus did.

Healing is the blessing of God offered to everyone who believes in Jesus. God wants you strong and healthy. Of course we are to care for our bodies well with a healthy diet, fresh air, and exercise, but if we get attacked with sickness, disease, or infirmity, we have promises we can stand on for our healing. Many have been healed through prayer ministry and by believing for God's intervention. God has also given wisdom to physicians so that we have practical tools as well.

Whether you are healed through supernatural or natural means, God is the source of your healing. Lean upon Him and seek His wisdom first when you need healing for your body. He will direct you in the steps to take. When you obey His leading, you can anticipate great results.

DECREES

I DECREE THAT:

1. God daily loads me with good benefits. My soul is blessed, my body is blessed, and I am free from all iniquities and sickness.

2. I am healthy and rejuvenated, getting stronger and energized daily.

3. I refresh myself every day in the Living Word that gives abundant life.

4. My health is restored to me, and I am healed of all wounds in my soul.

5. I am strengthened daily and drink of the joy of the Lord that strengthens me and brings me full emotional healing.

6. God takes pleasure in prospering me in my spirit, soul, and body.

7. Healing is the "children's bread"; therefore, I taste of the goodness of God and I am healed.

8. I am satisfied with longevity, and daily my health is renewed.

9. I am healthy in every way—spirit, soul (mind, will, emotions), and body—and I'm destined to prosper.

10. Strength and vigor possess my cells and organs. I live a righteous life that gives me power and offers nourishment to my bones.

Decrees based on the following Scriptures: Psalm 103:2–3; Job 33:25; Jeremiah 31:25; Matthew 11:28; Nehemiah 8:10; Luke 6:23; 3 John 2; Psalm 149:4; Proverbs 4:22; Proverbs 3:8

ACTIVATION

Get comfortable in a quiet place, close your eyes, and invite the Lord to fill you with a revelation of your body, soul, and spirit in optimum health and strength. Invite God's perfect health to fill each part of your body. You can even focus on certain organs if you like. I enjoy starting at the top of my head and going all the way down to my feet, inviting the Spirit to quicken my mortal body with His strength.

BLESSED WITH REJUVENATION

Bless the LORD, O my soul...
Who satisfies your years with good things,
So that your youth is renewed like the eagle.

PSALM 103:2A, 5

Many adults in our culture are concerned about aging. They worry about wrinkles, weight, energy levels, flabby skin, memory, and mental focus. There is also a mind-set in Western societies that suggests when a person enters his or her sixties, it is time to dial down, chill out, downsize, and live on limited retirement income.

The danger of this mentality is that our seniors who are in their prime, filled with wisdom and life experience, are opting out while there is so much for them to accomplish still. As a result, the next generation potentially loses the valuable unfulfilled accomplishments seniors carry, in addition to the new levels of wisdom they could have attained by continuing to live with fresh and progressive perspective.

The Bible speaks much about renewal. Abraham lived a full life and was rich in all things when he died at the ripe old age of one hundred and seventy-five. His wife Sarah was gorgeous in her older years and gave birth to her child in her nineties. Caleb at aged eighty-five was eager to fulfill prophetic destiny. Moses began to lead Israel through the wilderness in his eighties, and in his older years his eyes did not grow dim.

When we receive Christ, we are filled with eternal life. This is God's glorious life. You can have expectation to be renewed daily through the Word of God. God wants your strength, vitality, and beauty to be rejuvenated regularly.

A friend of mine had an acquaintance who was in his late seventies but he didn't look a day over fifty. He asked the man what his secret was, and the response was interesting. The man said he took communion every day and believed for supernatural rejuvenation. It certainly worked. I shared this with a friend who started the same regime, and it worked for her too. Her friends starting tell her how young she looked and asked where she got all her energy.

We do not need to buy into a lie that declares we will diminish in vitality and appearance as we age. We can always be fresh. As our days are, so shall our strength be! (Deuteronomy 33:25). We can always radiate the glory of the Lord. In fact, the Word reveals that, "The latter glory of this house will be greater than the former" (Haggai 2:9).

You are blessed with rejuvenation in Christ. Eternal life—"God life"—dwells within you. Rejoice and plan with expectation for a glorious future.

DECREES

I DECREE THAT:

1. I am refreshed and rejuvenated in the Lord. I am invigorated and renewed.
2. Every living cell in my body is rejuvenated.
3. I am empowered by the Lord in my inner man, and as a result I am full of vigor and vitality.
4. I receive age reversal as my youth is being renewed as the eagle.
5. I decree Christ in me is the hope of glory (bounty, splendor, majesty) for my body, soul, and spirit. I am filled with His glory.
6. I celebrate my salvation in Christ daily, and as a result I am rejuvenated, refreshed, and replenished.
7. As my days are, so shall my strength be.
8. I am ever strengthened and rejuvenated from "glory to glory."
9. I am blessed with eternal life activating daily in me.
10. I am renewed this day because the Holy Spirit is filling me with life and light.

*Decrees based on the following Scriptures: Psalm 103:2a, 5;
Psalm 45:13; Psalm 103:5; Colossians 1:27; Philippians 2:12;
Deuteronomy 33:25; 1 Peter 5:10; Haggai 2:9; John 4:14;
Romans 8:11*

ACTIVATION

Look in the mirror and proclaim with confidence the beauty, energy, renewed favor, and brightness of mind and vision that you carry in the Lord. Decree youthfulness with confidence and faith over that awesome person you see in the mirror.

_____

_____

_____

_____

_____

_____

_____

_____

_____

_____

BLESSED WITH FAITH

And without faith it is impossible to please Him, for he who comes to God must believe that He is and that He is a rewarder of those who seek Him.

HEBREWS 11:6

I like to think of faith as our God-given downloader and connector to His promises—to His divine glory. My first time in Las Vegas, a pastor took me and my ministry team to a buffet. I thought I had died and gone to heaven! It was the largest display of food I had ever seen. There were counters of salads, seafood, beef, chicken, turkey, ham, Asian food, Mexican food, Italian food, vegetables, breads and spreads, appetizers, desserts, and beverages. Everything was available to us once we passed through the entrance gate. The pastor had paid for our meal tickets so we could pass through.

At a buffet, the food is yours for the taking. It has been prepared, cooked, and presented, *but* it is up to you to fill your plate. A person could actually starve sitting in a buffet long enough if he or she does not fill a plate with the food available.

All the promises of God were given two thousand years

ago to everyone who believes. God has held nothing back. Ephesians 1:3 teaches that every spiritual blessing in the heavenly places has already been given to us. Second Peter 1:2–4 further confirms that we have been given everything that pertains to life and godliness and that all the exceedingly great and precious promises are already ours in Christ.

These promises are for every believer to enjoy. Jesus paid the "meal ticket" for our entrance into this divine buffet of promises and blessings through His death on the cross. They have all been prepared and made available for us, but we need to use our faith to "fill our plates." All the promises are to be appropriated into our lives by faith.

Hebrews 11:6 says that we cannot please God without faith. Habakkuk 2:4 teaches that the righteous lives by his faith. Faith is your connector to the promises. Faith is your spiritual downloader.

Jesus taught us that "all things are possible to him who believes" (Mark 9:23). Activate your faith daily and enjoy the manifestation of God's promises and blessings in your life.

DECREES

I DECREE THAT:

1. I have faith in God; therefore, when I speak to obstacles in my life, they move.

2. I rejoice and give thanks because faith in me is bearing much fruit.

3. I step out in bold faith with confidence, knowing that nothing is impossible for God.

4. As I walk in faith, I experience the things I have hoped for and the manifestation of what I believe.

5. Because I believe, God answers me even before the word is on my lips.

6. God takes pleasure in me because my faith pleases Him.

7. Through faith I call those things that are not, as though they are. By faith I call God's purposes into being.

8. All things are possible to me in Christ because I believe.

9. I commit all my ways to God in faith. I trust Him in everything.

10. I take up the shield of faith that quenches every fiery dart of the enemy that comes against me or my loved ones.

Decrees based on the following Scriptures: Mark 11:22; Ephesians 3:12; Hebrews 11:1–6; 1 Corinthians 16:13; Ezekiel 37:1–14; Isaiah 65:24; Luke 18:27; Psalm 37:5; Ephesians 6:16

ACTIVATION

Find some promises in the Scriptures that God has given to those who believe. Invite the Holy Spirit to make them personal to you. Meditate on them until they become secured within your heart as an "internal reality." When it is real within your heart, without doubt, that is faith.

Once you have embraced the promise and you know it is alive within you, apply it to a situation in your life. Stand in faith and wait for the results to manifest.

BLESSED WITH FREEDOM

It was for freedom that Christ set us free; therefore keep standing firm and do not be subject again to a yoke of slavery.

GALATIANS 5:1

Freedom is so glorious, and bondage is hellishly oppressive. You were created for freedom! Jesus came to set you free from sin, oppression, poverty, sickness, and disease. He wants you to enjoy the fullness of His freedom and liberty.

Before I received Jesus as my personal Savior, I engaged in practices that promised me a good time, peace, euphoria, and relationships. What was supposed to be good caused my life to spiral downhill into destruction. I was oppressed, suicidal, and without hope. That is bondage—slavery! Sin destroys!

The night I came to Christ, I tasted true freedom—true love! All the guilt, shame, and fear melted away, and my freedom-filled life began.

Unrighteousness binds and oppresses but so does self-righteousness. The apostle Paul gave warning to the church in Galatia. They had been set free by the love, grace, and power of Jesus Christ, yet then they attempted to be justified by the law.

My born-again experience was beautiful. I knew my

salvation and deliverance from bondage had nothing to do with my own righteousness or efforts. I had nothing good to offer the Lord, yet He delivered me into His liberty. I was bathed in the grace of God and passionately grew in my walk with the Lord. I was in love and I knew He loved me.

I had no grid for legalism, as I had never known it. I was delivered from unrighteousness to His righteousness via a miracle of His grace. It was all I knew.

Several years later, I was serving on the mission field not understanding how to rightly divide the Word in regard to grace versus the law. I had dedicated and faithful leaders, but they did not understand grace. They taught that God was upset with us when we sinned, and they were diligent to point out areas of my life that they felt were upsetting God.

I was devastated. The thought of hurting God was overwhelming to me. I never wanted to disappoint Him. I started to strive to "fix" myself. After five months of strenuous attempts to self-improve, I came to a conclusion: I was a failure, a complete disappointment to God. The more I tried, the more bound I became. My freedom and joy had vanished.

After returning from the field discouraged, the Lord revealed how His good news is to liberate and not bind or oppress. Jesus became my sin, bore my punishment, and liberated me from all debt I owed to God. This is good news! When the revelation hit, I wept, I laughed, and I praised. My freedom was restored.

Jesus came to give you freedom. Freedom to live for Him. Freedom to know Him. Freedom to love Him—and others.

It was for freedom that Christ has set you free!

DECREES

I DECREE THAT:

1. I have been set free from all oppression through Christ.
2. I rejoice in my God-given freedom. I am free indeed!
3. I am free to live; I am free to love; I am free to "be" in Christ.
4. I am free to run my race in life and finish strong.
5. I am free through Christ from the law of sin and death.
6. The Lord has set me free from my enemies.
7. My head has been lifted high above my enemies, and my feet are set upon the solid Rock.
8. The Spirit of the Lord lives in me and gives me liberty to love extravagantly.
9. I use my freedom to serve others.
10. Where the Spirit of the Lord is, there is freedom. The Spirit of liberty dwells richly in me!

Decrees based on the following Scriptures: Galatians 5:1; John 8:36; 2 Corinthians 3:17; Galatians 5:13–14; 1 Peter 2:16; 2 Corinthians 3:17

ACTIVATION

List any areas of your life that are oppressing you. Ask Him to give you a revelation of His grace and pray for deliverance from anything that is robbing you of your freedom in Christ.

_____

_____

_____

_____

_____

_____

_____

_____

_____

_____

_____

BLESSED WITH REST

Rest in the LORD and wait patiently for Him.

PSALM 37:7A

The natural physical body requires rest in order to replenish its strength, health, and vitality. Without rest, your physical organs and general health are taxed. Individuals who lack rest, lack energy and clarity of thought.

God wants you to live in His spiritual rest. When your spiritual rest is established, everything else functions better. Your spiritual well-being is your "core well-being."

God created the heavens and the earth and then rested on the seventh day. Yes, even God rested. In the law, He included the Sabbath—a day of rest. Jesus has become our Sabbath—our Eternal Rest.

When I began to preach publicly, I was often anxious. I wondered if I had the right message and if I was able to articulate it well. One night, prior to a speaking engagement scheduled for the next morning, I was worried and concerned. I had studied and prayed for weeks prior but did not sense I had a message. I couldn't sleep and was restless.

My husband exhorted me to relax and sleep, but I thought he was being insensitive. All night long I struggled, and in the morning I still did not have the message. In the midst of tears, the Lord spoke to me: "Why are you anxious? Go in My rest. I will give you the Word as you speak." I had to make a choice in that moment to enter His rest.

In response, I cast all my cares upon Him and chose to enter His rest. We drove to the church still not knowing what I was going to share, but I had entered rest. I was settled and trusted God to do what He said He would do.

The morning service was amazing, and at the end of the message the altar was full. That was not the last time God invited me to enter into His rest. He has everything under control and wants us to rest in Him regularly.

You will be strengthened and refreshed as you rest in Him.

DECREES

I DECREE THAT:

1. The presence of the Lord is with me, and He gives me rest; therefore, I am anxious for nothing.
2. When I feel heavy and burdened, I go to the Lord and He gives rest to my soul.
3. I am yoked to the Lord and experience rest in Him.
4. I am satisfied and at rest in the Lord.
5. The refreshing rest of the Lord fills me and grants me joy.
6. I walk in the good ways of the Lord and therefore find rest in life.
7. The Lord has lavished with me with bounty and has granted me rest.
8. God causes those around me to refresh me in spirit and soul.
9. I am at rest when evil surrounds me, as I am confident God will bring forth justice. He will keep me safe and at peace.
10. Jesus is my Sabbath. I abide in His rest.

Decrees based on the following Scriptures: Exodus 33:14; Philippians 4:6; Matthew 11:28–30; Jeremiah 31:25; Romans 15:32; Jeremiah 6:16; Exodus 31:17; Psalm 116:7; 1 Corinthians 16:18; Psalm 37:7; Psalm 91:10–15; Exodus 20:8

ACTIVATION

Find yourself a comfortable chair or bed and settle into a restful position. Take some deep breaths, letting all tension and anxiety go as you focus your mind on the goodness of God. Let Him absorb all that concerns you.

_____

_____

_____

_____

_____

_____

_____

_____

_____

_____

_____

DAY TWENTY-SEVEN

BLESSED WITH JOY

You will make known to me the path of life;
In Your presence is fullness of joy;
In Your right hand there are pleasures forever.

PSALM 16:11

I was driving back home with some friends after a week of successful missions outreach. Our hearts were elated as we reviewed all God had done in our midst. So many lives were deeply touched and transformed by His love, and we were full! We stopped for fuel and lunch, and all of a sudden the joy of the Lord hit us in such a huge way that none of us could stop laughing. Others in the restaurant entered the joy realm too.

This situation reminded me of Luke 10. The disciples had been sent out to minister the gospel and they returned excited. "The seventy returned with joy saying, 'Lord, even the demons are subject to us in Your name'" (v. 17). Jesus was elated for them: "At that very time He rejoiced greatly in the Holy Spirit…" (v. 21).

Joy is refreshing and empowering. It is glorious, and heaven is full of it. Yes, in the presence of the Lord there is fullness of joy!

Jesus is committed to you being filled with joy.

"These things I have spoken to you so that My joy may be in you, and that your joy may be made full" (John 15:11).

"Until now you have asked for nothing in My name; ask and you will receive, so that your joy may be made full" (John 16:24).

Imagine waking up every morning filled with joy. You go about your day and joy floods you in waves, and then when you lie down to sleep at night joy washes over your soul. That is a nice reflection, isn't it?

Many people are often filled with so much stress that they never experience joy. Life is so serious and heavy for them. This is not God's will for mankind. He wants everyone to experience the beauty of His joy. In Christ, you have been blessed with "joy unspeakable and full of glory."

Choose to receive His joy. Think on those things that are good and lovely, and allow your heart to engage in some pure joy.

DECREES

I DECREE THAT:

1. The joy of the Lord is my strength!
2. God has granted to me light, gladness, joy, and honor.
3. In the presence of the Lord there is fullness of joy. I dwell in His presence.
4. I will always experience joy in the Lord because I trust in Him.
5. Joy comes in the morning when I go through difficult and dark night seasons in my life.
6. When I am saddened or discouraged, the Lord restores the joy of my salvation.
7. God's desire for me is that my life is filled with joy.
8. The fruit of the Spirit is joy, and it is being produced in my life by His presence.
9. I count it all joy when I face testings, temptations, and trials, because God will produce wonderful things in me as I endure and overcome.
10. I rejoice in the Lord with joy unspeakable and full of glory.

Decrees based on the following Scriptures: Nehemiah 8:10; Esther 8:16; Psalm 16:11; Psalm 5:11; Psalm 30:5; Psalm 51:12; John 15:11; Galatians 5:22; James 1:2; 1 Peter 1:8

ACTIVATION

Make a list of things that bring you joy. Meditate on them and allow joy to fill you. Ask God to bring you into the fullness of His joy.

DAY TWENTY-EIGHT

BLESSED WITH KINGDOM AUTHORITY

And Jesus came up and spoke to them, saying,
"All authority has been given to Me in heaven and on earth.
Go therefore and make disciples of all the nations,
baptizing them in the name of the Father and the
Son and the Holy Spirit."

MATTHEW: 28:18–19

Jesus came to reveal His kingdom—the kingdom of heaven. It is an invisible spiritual kingdom, and yet we can see outward manifestations of this realm while living in the earth.

When you invite Jesus into your heart as Lord of your life, you become a citizen of this kingdom and you have full access to its benefits. In fact, the Bible teaches that you become an "ambassador" of this kingdom while living in the earth (2 Corinthians 5:20). Ambassadors represent the government of the nation they are from, in the nation to which they are sent. They are governed by the laws of the land they are from and not by the laws of the nation they are residing in.

You are living in the earth, representing the kingdom of heaven. You are God's ambassador and you are governed by

His royal laws of love. As His ambassador, you have Christ's authority to reach the world you live in with His love, light, and truth.

Jesus commissioned His disciples with authority to preach the good news of the kingdom and to heal the sick, raise the dead, cleanse the lepers, and free the oppressed (Matthew 10:1, 7–8; Mark 16:15–17). These are all expressions of His love.

You are also commissioned with His authority to represent Him in the earth. Jesus taught that those who believe would do the same works He did and even greater (John 14:12). This is how the world will come to know Him.

You have been given full access into this glorious kingdom, and you have been given authority through Christ to bring the manifestation of this kingdom into the earth. You rule and reign with Him, and your life makes a difference.

You have authority over all the works of the enemy (Luke 10:19). You have authority to work miracles on Christ's behalf. You are not just a mere human being; you are a heavenly being living in the earth. You are a supernatural being representing Christ, His kingdom, and His righteousness.

Go forth into your realm of influence and spread the wonderful news of His love and manifest His kingdom glory. You have been granted authority to do so.

DECREES

I DECREE THAT:

1. I am called as an ambassador of Christ to represent His kingdom in the earth.
2. The kingdom I serve is a kingdom that cannot be shaken.
3. I have authority over the power of the enemy.
4. In Christ I have authority to heal the sick, cast out devils, cleanse lepers, and raise the dead.
5. I have been given the keys of the kingdom, and whatever I bind in the earth shall have been bound in heaven. Whatever I loose shall have been loosed in heaven.
6. Jesus has given me the authority to forgive sins.
7. I have authority in Christ to go and make disciples of nations.
8. In Christ I can baptize in the name of the Father, the Son, and the Holy Spirit.
9. I have authority to go before the throne of grace with bold confidence to receive mercy and to find help in time of need.
10. I have authority to approach my heavenly Father and ask Him to bring His kingdom, will, and purposes into the earth.

Decrees based on the following Scriptures: 2 Corinthians 5:20; Hebrews 12:28; Luke 10:19; Matthew 10:1, 7–8; Mark 16:15–17; Matthew 16:19; John 20:23; Matthew 28:18–20; Hebrews 4:16; Matthew 6:10

ACTIVATION

Make a list of five situations in your realm of influence that need a touch from God. Then use your kingdom authority to speak light and life into those situations. With faith in the power of God, believe for a shift to take place. Praise the Lord for bringing forth the change, and watch for the results. Journal the progress.

BLESSED WITH AN OPEN HEAVEN

After being baptized, Jesus came up immediately from the water; and behold, the heavens were opened, and he saw the Spirit of God descending as a dove and lighting on Him.

MATTHEW 3:16

God's heaven is filled with love, joy, perfection, purity, peace, extravagance, health, prosperity, abundance, freedom, liberty, glory, and oh, so much more. Imagine yourself living under an open heaven with all those attributes falling on you like rain!

Two thousand years ago, Jesus opened the heavens for you at His water baptism. John's baptism in water was for repentance from sin. Jesus never sinned, so He did not need to partake of that baptism. John the Baptist knew this and that is why he struggled to baptize Him, but Jesus' response to John was: "Permit it at this time, for in this way it is fitting for us to fulfill all righteousness" (Matthew 3:15). Jesus was being baptized for you and "as you" for your repentance.

The glory of the gospel is that Jesus did everything for you and as you. He repented for you and as you. He died for you and as you. He paid the penalty for your sins and was raised from the dead into eternal life for you and as you. This is glorious news!

When Jesus came up out of the waters of baptism, the heavens were opened and they are still opened over Him—and He lives in you. This means that you can live under the open heaven all the days of your life. This is not because you deserve it but because He accomplished all that was needed for you to live under this great blessing.

Deuteronomy 28:12 declares one of the many blessings that will come upon believers. It is the blessing of the open heaven: "The Lord will open for you His good storehouse, the heavens, to give rain to your land in its season and to bless all the work of your hand; and you shall lend to many nations but you shall not borrow."

Wow, that is one loaded Scripture promise! Imagine what your life would be like if you were to live under the open heaven 24/7 with all the works of your hands being blessed. How wonderful!

All the promises are available to every believer, but they will only be experienced when you connect to them with your faith. Faith is your kingdom currency. Stir your faith to live under the open heaven. Jesus opened it especially for you!

DECREES

I DECREE THAT:

1. Christ Jesus opened the heavens for me two thousand years ago.
2. I live under an open heaven.
3. Heavenly blessings come upon me and overtake me.
4. I am blessed coming in and blessed going out.
5. The angels of God ascend and descend upon my life because Christ dwells within me.
6. I am the house of God, and Christ in me is the gate of heaven; therefore, I can release heavenly glory into the earth.
7. Heaven's rain (revival and blessings) falls upon me.
8. The Father favors me because Christ was baptized as me.
9. Heaven's atmosphere prevails like a glory cloud over my life.
10. I experience an open heaven everywhere I go and in whatever I do.

Decrees based on the following Scriptures: Matthew 3:13–17; Deuteronomy 28:1–12; Genesis 28:12–17; John 1:51

ACTIVATION

Daily decree the blessings of the open heaven over your home, family, finances, business, and spiritual walk. With intentionality look for the manifestations of God's blessings that visit you in these areas. Journal the results.

_____

_____

_____

_____

_____

_____

_____

_____

_____

_____

_____

_____

BLESSED WITH ANGELIC SERVICE

But to which of the angels has He ever said, "Sit at My right hand, until I make your enemies a footstool for your feet"? Are they not all ministering spirits, sent out to render service for the sake of those who will inherit salvation?

HEBREWS 1:13–14

All through the Bible, you will find evidence of angelic visitation and activity. Angels protect, bring messages, interact with mankind, worship, engage in warfare, and serve God's purposes and pleasure both in heaven and in earth.

If you are a believer, then you are surrounded by angels. The Bible says that they encamp around believers (Psalm 34:7). Even though you can't see them or sense them they are there.

In Bible history we discover that God in His sovereignty often chose to send angels with messages rather than deliver the message directly through His own Spirit. For example, He delivered a significant prophetic message to Mary the mother of Jesus regarding the conception of the Messiah by the Holy Spirit, through the angel Gabriel.

The word *angel* comes from the Greek word which means

"messenger," and in Hebrews 1:14 we discover that angels are "servants" sent by God to serve those who inherit salvation (believers in Christ).

In the New Testament we see angels heralding the birth of Jesus, appearing in dreams, bringing important messages, strengthening Jesus in the wilderness, leading the apostles out of prison, bringing sinners to hear the gospel, and being very involved in the events of the end of the age described in the book of Revelation.

This is a season of accelerated angelic visitation in the earth. One of your kingdom blessings is that God has assigned angels charge over you to guard you in all your ways (Psalm 91:11). This is so wonderful. You might not see them or sense them, but they are with you.

You are blessed with "invisible friends."

DECREES

I DECREE THAT:

1. I am watched over by God's angels.
2. Angels bring provision to me.
3. God commissions angels to bring messages to me like He did for Mary, Joseph, Zacharias, and others.
4. God sends His angels to purify me.
5. Angels are released into action when I proclaim the Word of God.
6. God has given His angels charge over me to protect me from harm.
7. God sends His angels to serve His purposes in me.
8. I am able to discern angels with the Holy Spirit's gift of the discerning of spirits.
9. Angels bring answers to prayer for me.
10. Angels are not to be worshiped, and they turn my attention to worship Jesus.

Decrees based on the following Scriptures: Psalm 91:11; 1 Kings 19:5–7; Luke 1; Isaiah 6:6–7; Psalm 103:20; Hebrews 11:1; Daniel 9:21–28; Revelation 19:10

ACTIVATION

Spend time worshiping God with a realization that angels are worshiping Him before the throne at the same time.

DAY THIRTY-ONE

BLESSED WITH A GLORIOUS FUTURE

"For I know the plans that I have for you," declares the LORD,
"plans for welfare and not for calamity to give you
a future and a hope."

JEREMIAH 29:11

In a day when there are economic, political, and natural environmental shakings, people are frightened concerning their future. Parents and grandparents are concerned for the next generation's well-being, individuals worry about their financial future, and the masses are generally feeling unsettled. Will there be enough food and water to sustain the world's population? Will terrorism prevail? Will war break out? Will the economy collapse? Will plagues, pestilence, earthquakes, or storms destroy our quality of life? These are very real questions that rattle the mind of many today.

God's promises of blessings for His people are not dependent on what is happening in the world around you. He has secured you into a glorious future with absolute confidence that your life will be good!

In the book of Exodus we find the Egyptians being visited by various plagues, but God's people were not touched by them. The Egyptians suffered a plague of darkness, but the

Israelites had light. They were living in the same area, but Israel was safe from what was affecting Egypt. When God led them out into the wilderness, they were concerned about what they were going to eat and drink, but God already had that looked after. He blessed them in the wilderness.

They had bread from heaven, water from the rock, and God's manifest presence in a cloud by day and in a pillar of fire by night. Their clothing never wore out. They had been slaves in Egypt, but now they did not have to work for their provision. It came supernaturally to them by the hand of God. They were extremely blessed and yet they remained in fear of their future.

Abraham experienced drought and war in his day, but it did not affect him. He was blessed by God in the midst of it. He left Egypt full, he won wars with his own army, and he was blessed with a miracle child. At the end of his life, he was rich in all things. He was blessed because God gave him a covenant of blessing. You have this same covenant in Christ.

You have been promised a glorious future no matter what is happening in the world around you. You are created to make a difference and to bring light into the darkness. You will influence the world, and the world will not influence you.

In Christ, you are actually a heavenly being living in the earth and not an earthly being trying to get into heaven. For sure there will be shakings in the earth, but God has promised to keep you in His blessings in the midst of it. He will bless you with His presence, goodness, protection, provision, and love. Jesus said that there would be tribulation in the world, but you could rejoice because He has overcome the world (John 16:33). He wants you to remember that although you are in the world, you are not of it (John 17:16). You are a heavenly child with a very glorious future! Live it to the full without fear.

DECREES

I DECREE THAT:

1. I have a glorious future in Christ.
2. I am full of hope when I think about my future.
3. I belong to the eternal kingdom of God, which will never be shaken.
4. The Lord protects me from all evil, all my days.
5. God sets a banquet before me in the presence of my enemies.
6. Goodness and mercy follow me all the days of my life.
7. No weapon formed against me shall prosper.
8. God works everything together for my good in every situation in life. I am a winner!
9. I am steadfast in the Lord, immovable, secure in His blessings.
10. God's glorious favor over my life fills all my days and is a shield around me, protecting me from evil.

Decrees based on the following Scriptures: Jeremiah 29:11; Hebrews 12:28; Psalm 121:7; Psalm 23:5–6; Isaiah 54:17; Romans 8:28; 1 Corinthians 15:58; Psalm 5:12

ACTIVATION

Take time today to soak in the Lord's presence and dream about your glorious future. Allow the Spirit of God to fill you with glimpses of His goodness that He has in store for the days ahead of you. Journal what you see and hear and then *believe*.

ABOUT THE AUTHOR

Patricia King has been a pioneering voice in Christian ministry for more than thirty years. She is an accomplished author, motivational speaker, media host, producer, and businesswoman. She is the founder and leader of Patricia King Ministries. To find out more, go to PatriciaKing.com. You can also connect with Patricia through her social media feeds on Facebook and Twitter.

NOTES

NOTES

NOTES

NOTES

NOTES